Morocco

Morocco

**BY ETTAGALE BLAUER
& JASON LAURÉ**

Enchantment of the World™
Second Series

CHILDREN'S PRESS®

An Imprint of Scholastic Inc.

Frontispiece: **Woman in Chefchaouen**

Consultant: Emilio Spadola, Associate Professor of Anthropology, Colgate University, Hamilton, New York
Please note: All statistics are as up-to-date as possible at the time of publication.

Book production by The Design Lab

Library of Congress Cataloging-in-Publication Data
Blauer, Ettagale.
 Morocco / by Ettagale Blauer and Jason Lauré.
    pages cm. — (Enchantment of the world)
 Includes bibliographical references and index.
 Audience: Grades 4–6.
 ISBN 978-0-531-21696-5 (library binding)
 1. Morocco—Juvenile literature. I. Lauré, Jason. II. Title.
 DT305.B53 2015
 964—dc23   2014046274

Acknowledgments
We thank the people of Morocco who were helpful at every turn on all our trips through their country, particularly through the changing political and cultural environments. We thank especially Consul General Mohammed Benabdeljalil, Chakib Ghadouani, director of the Moroccan National Tourist Office in New York, and Del Blaoui. We thank Noufissa Bernikhou for her rich and detailed insights into modern Moroccan life and culture.

Market in Marrakech

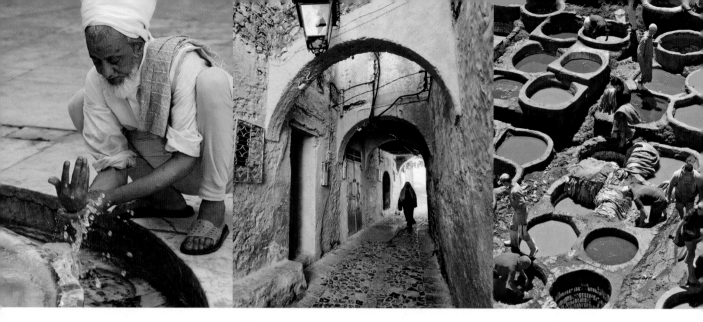

Contents

CHAPTER 1   A Modern Kingdom **8**

CHAPTER 2   Ocean, Mountain, Desert **14**

CHAPTER 3   Natural Life **26**

CHAPTER 4   Ancient Land, Modern Nation **34**

CHAPTER 5   Ruling the Kingdom **58**

CHAPTER 6 On the Job **70**

CHAPTER 7 People and Languages **86**

CHAPTER 8 Life of the Spirit **98**

CHAPTER 9 Arts and Sports **108**

CHAPTER 10 Daily Life **116**

Timeline **128**

Fast Facts **130**

To Find Out More **134**

Index **136**

Left to right: **Ritual purification, Chefchaouen, leather tanneries, High Atlas Mountains, Sahara**

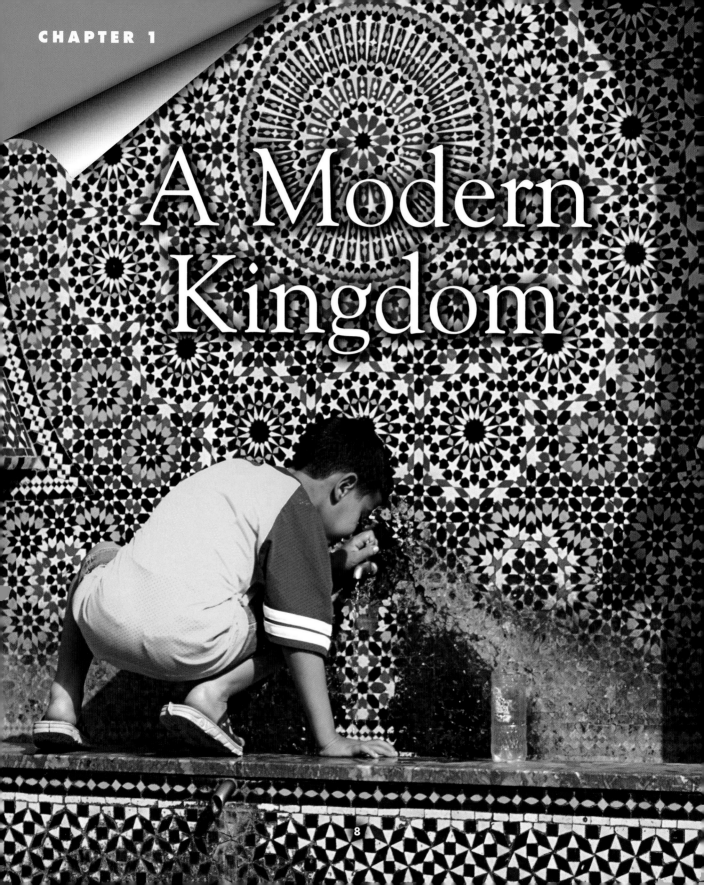

CHAPTER 1

A Modern Kingdom

THE KINGDOM OF MOROCCO OWES MUCH OF ITS history and culture to its location. Lying in northwestern Africa, Morocco is closer to Europe than any other African nation. The coast of Spain lies just 8.5 miles (13.7 kilometers) across the Strait of Gibraltar from the Moroccan city of Tangier. Africa, Europe, and the Middle East have all helped create the nation of Morocco, which has a rich mix of geography, cultures, history, and architecture.

Morocco features beautiful beaches, rugged mountains, and a wide swath of the Sahara, the largest desert on earth. Although Morocco is part of North Africa, its cultures and official religion, Islam, have more in common with the Arab nations of the Middle East than with the African cultures of central and southern Africa. Bordering both the Atlantic Ocean and the Mediterranean Sea, it has absorbed influences from around the Mediterranean and North Africa.

Opposite: **A boy drinks from a highly decorated fountain in Meknès. Morocco is renowned for its elaborate tile work.**

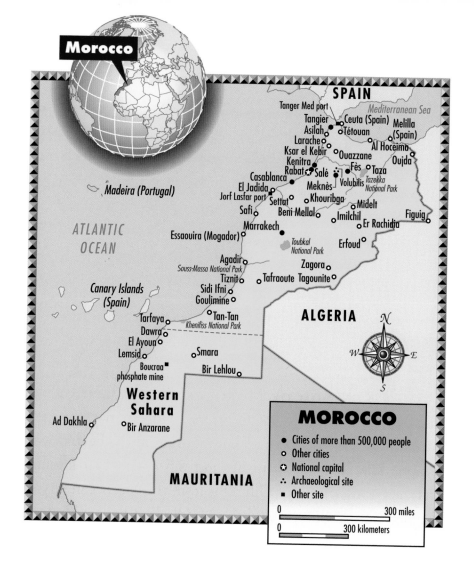

Morocco's rich history is evident throughout the country. People live, work, and shop in buildings that are hundreds of years old. The cities of Morocco are built upon a lively mix of ideas and backgrounds. They combine Islamic design, which features plentiful arches, colorful tiles, and geometric design, with Western architecture, busy Arab bazaars, and delicious foods. Cities such as Fès, Marrakech, and Tangier hold both the nation's rich past and its lively present, attracting visitors from around the world. By exploring the cities on foot, walking through the mazelike passageways, people can catch a glimpse into each city's unique personality.

Although Morocco is an ancient country, as a modern nation, it is relatively young. In the nineteenth century, much of it came under the control of France, while Spain controlled other parts. Morocco only became independent in 1956. Since then, Morocco has been ruled by a king, a member of the Alawite family.

Morocco's current king is Mohammed VI, who ascended to the throne in 1999, upon the death of his father, Hassan II. The king is putting a progressive stamp on every aspect of life in the country. He has pushed for improved educational

Colorful spices are piled high in a market in Marrakech.

standards, for new investment in the economy, for new roads and better airports, and for cultural changes that make life better for the people.

Mohammed VI has led the nation through difficult times in recent years. On December 18, 2010, an incident in the North African nation of Tunisia sparked an explosion of rage. The people were protesting the rigid rulers who controlled their lives. Known as the Arab Spring, the revolts quickly spread to neighboring Algeria and Egypt. Violence in the streets turned to political upheavals and several heads of state

During the Arab Spring, Moroccan protesters filled the streets of Rabat and other cities, demanding changes in the government.

were thrown out of office. Although protests in Morocco were not nearly as violent or widespread as in neighboring nations, Mohammed VI took steps to ease the tensions in Morocco. He made changes in the constitution that addressed some of the protesters' concerns. Morocco, however, has always been a more open society than its North African neighbors.

One of the biggest challenges Mohammed VI faces is the large number of unemployed young people who are desperate to find work. Equally challenging is the change in Morocco's climate as a result of global climate change. Hotter and drier conditions are already changing the nation's agriculture, one of its principal sources of both food and employment. These are the issues that will put Mohammed VI's ideas and leadership to the test. The changes and improvements he has made already suggest that Morocco, a nation with an ancient past, also has a promising future.

Boys share a laugh in Tétouan, a city in northern Morocco. Once they grow up, many boys leave Morocco in search of work. Most go to France.

CHAPTER 2

Ocean, Mountain, Desert

MOROCCO IS A LONG, NARROW COUNTRY located in northwestern Africa. It is bordered by the Atlantic Ocean to the west and the Mediterranean Sea to the north. Algeria lies to the east and southeast, and a disputed territory known as Western Sahara lies to the south. Morocco also borders the Spanish cities of Ceuta and Melilla, which lie on Africa's Mediterranean coast.

Morocco's land area covers 170,773 square miles (442,300 square kilometers), making it about the size of the U.S. state of California. Morocco has had control of much of Western Sahara since the 1970s. When the Western Sahara territory is included, Morocco's size grows by 103,000 square miles (266,000 sq km).

Opposite: **The Sahara spreads across most of North Africa, including Morocco. This vast desert is nearly as large as the entire United States.**

The Lay of the Land

Morocco's terrain is marked by extremes. Four mountain ranges cross the nation, running roughly northeast to southwest. The Rif Mountains are the northernmost chain, rising not far from the Mediterranean coast. Most of the peaks in the Rif Mountains

Spain in Morocco

After Morocco gained its independence, the crescent-shaped land held by Spain on Morocco's northern coast shrank to two small cities, Ceuta in the west and Melilla (below) in the east. Morocco surrounds them on three sides; the Mediterranean Sea forms the fourth border.

Ceuta is shaped somewhat like a hook protruding from the Moroccan mainland. It has been considered a part of Spain for five hundred years. About eighty-four thousand people live in the tiny city. Melilla, on the northeast Moroccan coast, has also been in Spanish hands for five hundred years. It has a population of about seventy-eight thousand people. Most residents of both cities are ethnically Spanish.

Both cities look across the Mediterranean to Spain and are connected to it by ferries. Spain has clung to these two territories, claiming they are part of the mother country. This has created unintended consequences. For example, anyone who sets foot in either Ceuta or Melilla is considered to be in Spain and can travel to the Spanish mainland freely without a passport. Many Africans are trying to reach Europe by any means possible to look for work, and Ceuta and Melilla have become major routes for migrants.

Spain has tried to repel the would-be migrants by building fences around Ceuta and Melilla. But no matter how high the fences, the migrants climb over them. The migrants risk their lives in many ways, sometimes even trying to swim around barriers that protrude from the cities into the Mediterranean Sea.

reach about 5,000 feet (1,500 meters). The range's tallest peak, Mount Tidirhine, has an elevation of 8,058 feet (2,456 m). The Rif Mountains act as a natural barrier that protects Morocco's Mediterranean coast and the port city of Tangier from the hot, dry winds that blow from the Sahara, a vast desert region that

The Laou River cuts through the Rif Mountains, forming a stunning gorge.

Morocco's Geographic Features

Area: 170,773 square miles (442,300 sq km)

Area Including Western Sahara: 273,773 square miles (709,000 sq km)

Highest Elevation: Mount Toubkal, 13,665 feet (4,165 m)

Lowest Elevation: Sebkha Tah, 180 feet (55 m) below sea level

Longest River: Draa, 683 miles (1,100 km)

Average High Temperature: In Rabat, 81°F (27°C) in July, 63°F (17°C) in January; in Marrakech, 101°F (38°C) in July, 66°F (19°C) in January

Average Low Temperature: In Rabat, 64°F (18°C) in July, 45°F (7°C) in January; in Marrakech, 70°F (21°C) in July, 44°F (6°C) in January

Wettest Region: Rif Mountains, 30 to 60 inches (80 to 150 cm) of rain annually

Driest Region: Sahara, less than 3 inches (8 cm) of rain annually

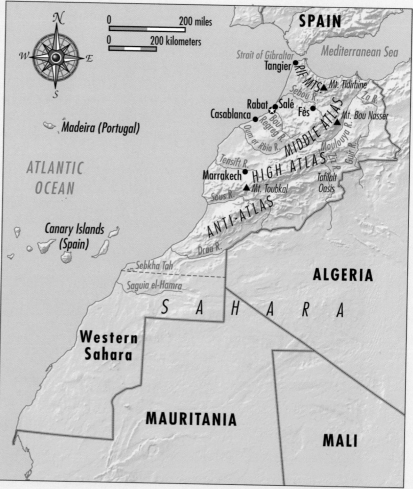

Fruit trees fill a field near the Sebou River.

spreads across much of North Africa. These mountains were once thickly forested, but in recent years, local villagers have cut down trees to make room to plant crops.

South of the Rif Mountains along the Atlantic coast lies a fertile plain, the site of some of Morocco's most productive agricultural land. The Sebou River runs through the plain, providing irrigation for the rice, strawberries, olives, and other plants that are grown there. More westerly parts of the coast, however, receive less rain. Sebkha Tah, the lowest point in

The striking, sculpted Anti-Atlas Mountains rise in southwestern Morocco.

Morocco at 180 feet (55 m) below sea level, is a natural basin in an arid region near the coastal city of Tarfaya.

Farther south are the three mountain chains that make up the Atlas Mountains. The Middle Atlas is the northeasternmost of the three chains. Its name comes from its height rather than location. Many peaks in the Middle Atlas top 8,000 feet (2,400 m). Its highest point is Mount Bou Nasser, at 10,958 feet (3,340 m). Most of Morocco's major cities lie in the temperate zone to the north of these mountains.

The High Atlas runs from the Atlantic across the middle of the country. This is Morocco's highest mountain range and includes the nation's highest point, Mount Toubkal, which soars to 13,665 feet (4,165 m). The northern flanks of the High Atlas are forested with trees such as cedar, pine, and cork, while the southern side, exposed to a hotter, drier climate, is barren. These towering mountains protect the fertile lands in the northern part of the country from the hot, dry winds and blowing sands of the Moroccan Sahara.

The Anti-Atlas chain lies to the west and south of the High Atlas. These dramatic arid mountains serve as the final barrier between the moderate climate of the north and the Sahara to the south.

The vast, desolate Sahara spreads out south of the Atlas Mountains. The Sahara stretches approximately 3,000 miles (4,800 km) across all of North Africa. It covers about 3,500,000 square miles (9,000,000 sq km), making it roughly the same size as the United States. Some parts of the Sahara are rocky, and much of it is made of flat, dusty land. Elsewhere are towering sand dunes. Most of the Moroccan Sahara receives less than 3 inches (8 centimeters) of rain per year, and temperatures frequently top 100 degrees Fahrenheit (38 degrees Celsius).

Mountains of Sand

Morocco has many dramatic geographic features, including great mountain ranges and beautiful beaches, but among its most impressive features are the towering sand dunes of the Sahara. Dunes are like living creatures, constantly changing as the wind pushes the grains of sand up over the top of the dune. Footsteps quickly disappear on a sand dune, erased by the endless winds. Although many people think of sand dunes when they think of deserts, most desert land is not covered with dunes. Sand dunes make up only about 10 percent of the Sahara.

Water in the Desert

An oasis is a place in the desert where water is available from underground springs or wells. An oasis is a vital lifeline in desert regions such as the Moroccan Sahara. It makes travel across the desert possible, but only for those people who have a keen sense of the geography of the region. Oases also provide watering holes for camels, the only creatures suited to life in the desert.

Moroccans can grow date palm trees and other crops in oases by using the oasis water to irrigate the land. People who depend on an oasis for their survival are careful with the water resources they have. In oases, the precious water is directed into underground channels and used sparingly. The farmers in these areas use drip irrigation, which feeds the trees slowly but constantly. This is a traditional system, well suited to the climate. People do not spray the water into the air, because most of it would evaporate and be wasted.

Some oases support only a few dozen date palm trees, but in the oasis at Figuig, near the border with Algeria, two hundred thousand palm trees stretch out in

Looking at Morocco's Cities

The largest city in Morocco is Casablanca (below), which in 2014 had an estimated population of 3,145,000. The site of Casablanca, which lies on the Atlantic coast, was settled as far back as the seventh century BCE. The city grew to be a wealthy port and then a base for pirates. During the French protectorate of the early twentieth century, the city grew quickly. Many French colonial buildings still stand, reminding visitors of the city's past. Today, Casablanca is Morocco's major port, as well as a financial and industrial center. Rabat, the nation's capital, is Morocco's second-largest city with a population of 1,656,000.

The nation's third-largest city, home to about 965,000 people, is Fès, also spelled Fez. The city is located near the Middle Atlas in the northeastern part of the country. Founded in 789 CE, Fès was an early capital of the kingdom and by the 1300s was a center of religious learning. Today, Fès includes two old

walled cities that continue to thrive, filled with homes, mosques, inns, and shops. Major sites include the Qarawiyin Mosque. Founded in 859, it is the oldest mosque in North Africa. Many traditional goods such as pottery and leatherwork are made in Fès.

Salé is the fourth-largest city, with a population of 903,000. Founded in the tenth century, for a time it was a wealthy port. Today, it is a suburb of Rabat.

Morocco's fifth-largest city, Marrakech, is home to about 839,000 people. Marrakech is known as the red or pink city because of the color of the earth used to build its walls. It is also known as the gateway to the Sahara. At the heart of the city lies the public square called Djemma el-Fna, which teems with shoppers, food, musicians, and tourists. The Koutoubia Mosque (above), built in the twelfth century, is one of the city's most visible landmarks. Marrakech boasts a well-preserved Jewish quarter called the Mellah. The city is filled with bustling souks, or markets, and peaceful gardens. Tourism, trade, and crafts are all important to the economy.

The snowcapped High Atlas Mountains rise behind Marrakech.

neat rows. Tafilalt, in southeastern Morocco, may be the largest oasis in the world. It is known for its high-quality dates, which were already being cultivated nearly one thousand years ago. Today, the oasis is a welcome sight for travelers after a strenuous trip across the Atlas Mountains.

Climate

Much of northern Morocco has a Mediterranean climate. This means it has hot, dry summers and mild, wet winters. The northeastern coastal region has some of the mildest weather. The city of Rabat, for example, has an average high temperature of 81°F (27°C) in July. Farther inland, however, temperatures increase, and in the desert, the temperature sometimes soars to

120°F (49°C) or more. Meanwhile, some of the towering Atlas Mountains are capped with snow for much of the year.

In recent decades, the average temperature around the globe has increased. This increase makes some regions hotter and drier, while increasing storm activity in other areas. This can make growing crops even more difficult in Morocco. Heavy downpours are not useful to farmers because the rainwater runs off the farmland quickly before the parched soil can absorb it. Torrential rains also wash away soil on slopes and hillsides, killing plants. Plants also die when there is no rain for a long period of time. Without the plant roots to hold the soil in place, the wind picks up the fertile topsoil and carries it away. When this happens, the land is no longer suitable for farming. To combat the loss of farmland from the drier climate, the Moroccan government is having one million date palm trees planted. These trees will help stabilize the soil and provide shade, lowering the temperature in the regions where they are planted.

Deadly Earthquakes

Morocco has occasionally suffered devastating damage from earthquakes. The northern region of Morocco was rocked by a 6.5 magnitude earthquake in February 2004. The port city of Al Hoceima was at the center of the quake, in which more than five hundred people died.

The deadliest quake known to have hit the region shook the coastal city of Agadir in 1960. The magnitude 5.7 quake caused more than twelve thousand deaths.

Ocean, Mountain, Desert **25**

CHAPTER 3

Natural Life

WITH ITS VARIED GEOGRAPHY, MOROCCO IS HOME to many different types of wildlife. Even in the hot, dry desert, some creatures are well adapted to tolerate the difficult conditions. The fennec fox makes its home in the Sahara. This small creature is renowned for its huge ears. These ears help the fennec fox keep its body cool by releasing a lot of heat into the air.

Similarly, the tiny jerboa also has huge ears. This little creature hops like a kangaroo but is in fact related to a mouse. Other creatures found in the desert include gerbils, snakes, lizards, and the tiny desert hedgehog.

Opposite: **The fennec fox has large ears and excellent hearing that enable it to hear its prey moving underground. The fennec's main foods are insects and small mammals.**

At Home in the Desert

No animal is better suited to desert life than the camel. The camel's gait can be deceptive. It seems to be strolling along, but thanks to its long legs, the camel is actually covering a lot of ground. Its wide hooves are perfectly designed to prevent it from sinking into the sand and for plodding across rocky terrain. When the desert sand starts to blow, a camel can close its third, transparent eyelids that protect the eyes but still allow the animal to see. The creature's hump can store up to 80 pounds (36 kilograms) of fat. When needed, the camel draws on that fat, which breaks down into water and energy. A fully grown camel can stand 7 feet (2 m) high at the hump and weigh up to 1,600 pounds (725 kg).

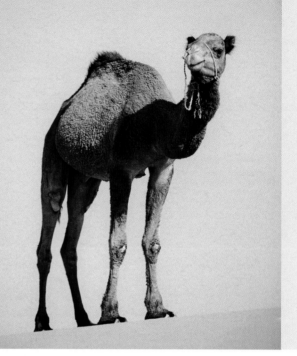

Wildlife of the Mountains and Coast

Many different species live in the mountains of Morocco. The Barbary macaque is the only monkey species to live in North Africa. It has a thick fur coat that protects it from the fierce cold of the Middle Atlas. It is not unusual to see Barbary macaques relaxing in the snow. It is estimated that only six thousand of the species survive in the wild, most in Morocco. Other creatures in the mountains include panthers, wild boars, Barbary sheep, and Cuvier's gazelle, a type of antelope with long ears and ribbed horns. The Atlas Mountains are also home to genets, carnivorous animals with long, striped tails and dramatic spots.

Morocco's long Atlantic coastline is home to many sea creatures such as dolphins and porpoises. The waters along the

A Symbol of the Nation

With its long, majestic mane, the Barbary lion is a national symbol of Morocco. Less well known than its East African cousins, it was one of the largest of all types of lions. The Barbary lion once roamed the Atlas Mountains, but it was a prime target for hunters and is now extinct in the wild. Many Barbary lions were also captured, so it is possible that some Barbary lions remain alive in zoos today.

Mediterranean coast are home to a shrinking population of Mediterranean monk seals, which are now thought to number fewer than six hundred.

About five thousand Barbary macaques live in Morocco.

Flamingos stop at a lagoon in southern Morocco.

Birdlife

More than 450 different species of birds have been seen in Morocco. Birdlife is particularly rich along the Atlantic Ocean. Species found there include Moroccan cormorants

For the Birds

The location of spectacular Souss-Massa National Park, near the city of Agadir, makes it a perfect home for a multitude of bird species. The park offers a variety of habitats for wildlife, ranging from sand dunes to rocky cliffs to dense forests. Among the bird species spotted here are falcons, eagles, spoonbill cranes, purple herons, and swallows. One of the park's standout sights is the rare northern bald ibis, a large black bird with a long red bill. Only a few hundred of these birds are living today, most in Morocco. Through careful conservation, the park has been increasing the population of northern bald ibises. The park's birds share the area with four-legged creatures, including jackals, red foxes, weasels, and African wildcats.

and sandwich terns. Migrating birds that travel from Europe during the winter include ducks, storks, and pelicans. Many can be found in Souss-Massa National Park.

Many birds also make their homes in the desert. The Egyptian nightjar has tan feathers that blend with the colors of the desert. It takes flight as the sun goes down, catching moths and other insects that are active at that time. When the Egyptian nightjar is ready to breed, it does not build a nest. Instead, it digs a shallow hole in the soil and lays its eggs there. Other desert species include scrub warblers, African desert warblers, and Dupont's larks.

With its sand-colored feathers, the Egyptian nightjar can be difficult to see as it roosts on the ground.

Acacia are among the few types of trees that can survive in the dry, rocky regions of Morocco.

Plant Life

About 11 percent of the land in Morocco is forested. The types of plants that grow in different regions of the country vary tremendously with rainfall. Along the coast are dry scrublands, where plants such as cork oak, acacia, heather, and honeysuckle grow. Forests of oaks, firs, or cedars grow on mountain slopes that receive abundant rain. Juniper and Aleppo pine are more common in dry mountain areas. Few plants grow in the Sahara, and those that do tend to be low to the ground. These include shrubs such as buffelgrass and Mediterranean saltbush. Moroccans have planted date palm trees and many other crops in the desert oases.

In the Garden

For people who live in a country with a hot, dry climate, gardens can be cool retreats from the sun as well as places to enjoy flowers and trees. But given Morocco's climate, it takes a lot of work to maintain a garden that looks natural. Gardens also require water, a scarce resource in Morocco. Gardeners choose plants that are best suited for the sunny, dry climate.

Marrakech, on the edge of the Sahara, is home to the Majorelle Garden (right). The garden is named for a French painter, Jacques Majorelle, who spent forty years creating this peaceful place filled with greenery. It is a perfect contrast to the red clay buildings of Marrakech. The garden is laced with streams and pools, which sport water lilies and lotus flowers. The cool, green environment attracts birds that stop for a drink of water and a break from the intense sun. Earthen walls protect the garden from the hot, dry winds and block out the sounds of the city just outside. Majorelle's brilliant blue house has been restored and now contains the Museum of Islamic Art.

The Mendoubia Gardens (below) in Tangier are located near the city's grand market. There is a dramatic contrast between the bustling, noisy market and the peaceful beauty of the gardens. An archway marks the entrance to the gardens, where visitors will see an eight-hundred-year-old banyan tree. This large tree has multiple trunks. Less peaceful looking are the seventeenth-century bronze cannons, reminders of the battles that have been fought to conquer this region.

CHAPTER 4

Ancient Land, Modern Nation

SOME OF MOROCCO'S EARLIEST HISTORY CAN BE read in fossils called trilobites. These are the remains of extinct ocean animals that are distant relations to the horseshoe crab. Some trilobite fossils have been dated back to the Cambrian period, about five hundred million years ago. At that time, North Africa was covered with a shallow sea, and trilobites were among the many creatures that lived in it. Many trilobite fossils are being found around Erfoud, an oasis in the southeast.

The ancestors of *Homo sapiens*, the human species that exists today, lived four hundred thousand years ago in what is now Morocco. Bones of human ancestors have been discovered in Salé, a town across the river from Rabat. The remains of early *Homo sapiens* show that modern humans have been living in the region for at least 160,000 years. This means that food and water were available in the region in prehistoric times.

Opposite: **A man holds a trilobite fossil found in Erfoud.**

Migrations

Amazigh people, sometimes known as Berbers, arrived about four thousand years ago in what is now Morocco. Having migrated from farther east, they are the ancestors of a large part of Morocco's population today.

About 2,800 years ago, Phoenicians, whose civilization was centered in the eastern Mediterranean, arrived on the Moroccan coast and made their way into the interior. The Phoenicians were great traders, and they came for salt, a crucial element in the preservation of food before the invention of

The Phoenicians established a number of settlements in Morocco, where they could anchor their boats and trade with Africans.

The Romans spread their art and culture throughout their empire. They often decorated their buildings in mosaics, pictures made of tiles. This mosaic of a woman playing a flute is in Volubilis, Morocco.

refrigeration. In about the sixth century BCE, the Phoenicians built settlements in the region, including one at Mogador, now called Essaouira, along the southern Moroccan coast.

By 300 BCE, some Amazigh people had established an independent kingdom that covered much of what is now northern Morocco. But the Roman Empire, which had spread across vast stretches of southern Europe and northern Africa by this time, gained control of this kingdom early in the first century CE.

People in the region followed a variety of religions at this time. Much of the population adopted the new religion of Christianity in the early centuries after it was founded about two thousand years ago. A sizable Jewish population also existed in the region. This would change dramatically with the introduction of Islam, a new religion that had begun on the Arabian Peninsula to the east.

Volubilis

Morocco's complex past comes alive in the ruins of the ancient city of Volubilis, located near the city of Meknès. Volubilis, founded in the third century BCE, was one of the most distant parts of the Roman Empire. The remains of the city reveal much about the lives of the people who lived there. The city included public baths and well-heated and well-cooled homes with finely detailed mosaic floors. Mosaics are designs created from tiny pieces of colored tiles. Even after two thousand years, some of the mosaics are as bright as they were the day they were made. Much of the region's wealth came from the olive groves planted nearby. Olives are pressed into oil and used in cooking. One of the principal buildings in Volubilis was an olive press. Over the course of a thousand years, people from many different cultures lived in Volubilis. During the late eighth century, it served briefly as the capital of Morocco under the rule of Idris ibn Abdallah, or Idris I.

When Idris moved the capital to Fès, Volubilis was abandoned. The buildings were so well constructed that they remained largely intact until an enormous earthquake hit in 1755. Today, what remains of Volubilis is carefully preserved.

By the eighth century, Arabs had moved into North Africa, bringing both their culture and their religion. Years of conflict between the Arabs and the Amazigh people followed. The Amazigh people, who lived in the rugged and isolated mountains, converted to Islam but merged it with their customary laws and beliefs.

Changing Hands

As more people converted to Islam, different groups sometimes came into conflict, and those who lost sometimes fled their homelands. One person who fled was Idris ibn Abdallah, who left the Arabian Peninsula and ended up in Morocco, where he began the Idrisid dynasty in 789 and became known as Idris I. His son, Idris II, founded the city of Fès, making it his capital. Around the same time, some Amazigh people established a distant settlement in southeastern Morocco, creating a gateway for trade across the Sahara. Though the Sahara can seem impassible, it has long been a trading route for the peoples of Africa who knew where to find the desert oases. They also knew how to use the stars to navigate through the Sahara, which has few landmarks on the ground. Amazigh traders reached as far as today's nation of Ghana, which was known as an important producer of gold.

Some Amazigh people used camels to travel across the Sahara.

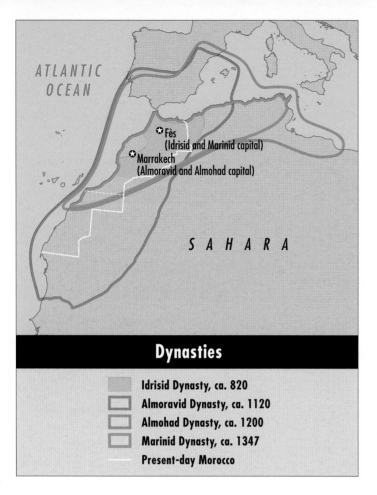

ATLANTIC
OCEAN

❂ Fès
(Idrisid and Marinid capital)
❂ Marrakech
(Almoravid and Almohad capital)

S A H A R A

Dynasties

Idrisid Dynasty, ca. 820
Almoravid Dynasty, ca. 1120
Almohad Dynasty, ca. 1200
Marinid Dynasty, ca. 1347
Present-day Morocco

The centuries following the establishment of the Idris dynasty saw the rise of various dynasties in the Atlas Mountains. These dynasties grew as they absorbed people ruled by other leaders in the north. Although the Amazigh peoples thought they would create a vast and unified political entity, this was not to be. The Amazigh peoples are known for their fierce independence. This helped them to survive and flourish amid the harsh climates of the rugged mountains, but it worked against them when they had to choose one group to rule others.

Eventually, the Almoravid dynasty emerged from the Sahara to unify Morocco, ruling from about 1060 to 1147. Known for their rigorous religious fervor, the Almoravids were also powerful allies of the Christians in southern Spain. Almoravid rule came to an end when another group, called the Almohads, conquered Marrakech on the edge of the Sahara.

Wave after wave of conquerors rolled through Morocco, claiming and then losing power. In the thirteenth century, the Marinids spread out from eastern Morocco to conquer the Almohads and gain control of Morocco. They ruled for some two hundred years. In the 1400s, the Portuguese arrived along

Morocco's Atlantic coast. Although the Portuguese were great sailors, they were not able to maintain control of any of Morocco's coastal towns.

The Alawite Dynasty

The Alawite dynasty, which continues to this day, took power in the mid-seventeenth century under Mawlay (Prince) al-Rashid. The Alawites encouraged trade throughout Africa as well as with Europe and the Middle East. When al-Rashid died

This fifteenth-century Portuguese tapestry depicts Portuguese troops entering Tangier in the mid-1400s.

in 1672, his half brother Mawlay Ismail ibn Sharif became the leader. Ismail was a brutal ruler. He organized a huge army, using enslaved soldiers from south of the Sahara. He terrified the local populations and warred constantly against Amazigh peoples, killing their leaders. Although Ismail was ruthless, he also had a vision for Morocco. Under his rule, an ambitious building program took place. Palaces, bridges, and protected, enclosed living areas called casbahs were erected. He ordered the construction of towns and ports and was particularly devoted to building in Meknès, the city in northern Morocco that served as his capital. There is little evidence of all this work today, largely because much of the new construction crumbled when the region was hit by a hurricane during Ismail's lifetime. Ismail did not plan for a future ruler, and as a result Meknès faded further after his death in 1727, because the rulers who followed him chose Fès and Marrakech as their capital cities instead.

Ismail is buried in a lavish tomb in Meknès.

In 1777, during the rule of Mohammed III, Morocco became the first nation in the world to officially recognize the newly independent United States of America. Morocco gave the United States a building in the old city of Tangier to house the offices of the U.S. diplomatic representatives, called a legation. This building still stands today and now houses the Tangier American Legation Museum.

Scramble for Africa

Morocco soon faced new challenges. In the late 1800s, France, Spain, Portugal, Germany, Belgium, and the United Kingdom began claiming vast territories on the African continent. They were eager to exploit the region's resources and the labor of its people. France and Spain battled for control of northern Africa.

This competition among European nations was known as the Scramble for Africa. As the Europeans fought over Africa, tensions grew. In an effort to prevent the conflict from turning into war, representatives from several European nations gathered at a conference in Berlin, Germany, in 1884. They agreed to respect each other's claims on African territories. Through this process, France gained

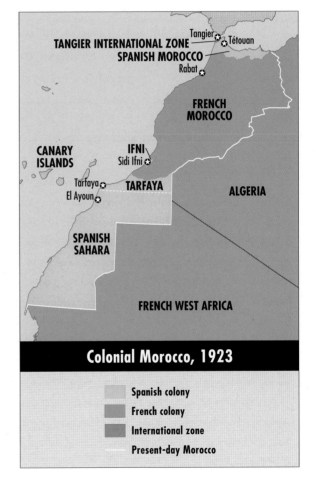

Colonial Morocco, 1923

Spanish colony
French colony
International zone
Present-day Morocco

effective control over most of Morocco, while Spain staked out portions of northern Morocco and the vast southern region that became known as Spanish Sahara.

In 1912, France proclaimed a protectorate over the parts of Morocco that it controlled. Under the protectorate, France gained some control over Morocco while agreeing to offer it protection. The leadership that followed was a combination of Moroccan royalty and French bureaucracy. The French tried to increase their control and influence in Morocco by bringing in French settlers to run the territory. After the protectorate was declared, many thousands of European colonists moved to Morocco.

The International City

During the French protectorate, Tangier was unique among Moroccan cities. Located on the Mediterranean Sea near the Strait of Gibraltar, Tangier had long been an important trading center. The Phoenicians were working out of Tangier at least 2,500 years ago, and many other cultures followed. By modern times, several European nations were eager to gain control of the port. In 1923, they worked out a deal that turned Tangier into the International Zone. It was administered by France, Spain, and Great Britain, with other nations joining later. Tangier, which was already very diverse and had a large Jewish population, became even more multicultural. Tangier remained an international city until 1956, when it was reintegrated into Morocco. Today, the city is home to about seven hundred thousand people. It continues to be a major port, has grown as an industrial center, and is renowned for its leatherwork, textiles, and silver goods.

Resistance and War

Strong Amazigh leaders fiercely resisted French rule, and France and Spain sent in legions of soldiers. Although the Amazigh independence fighters were loosely organized, they had many advantages over the Europeans, being very much at home in the Rif Mountains, where they had plenty of support and resources. They proved very difficult to defeat. It took four hundred thousand French and Spanish troops to subdue an Amazigh uprising in 1926.

Many Moroccans continued to desire full independence from their European rulers. Mohammed V, the Moroccan sultan, or king, backed this movement even though the French had installed him in his position in 1927.

European troops battle Amazigh rebel fighters during the Rif War.

Mohammed V

Independent, modern Morocco owes much to Mohammed Ben Youssef, also known as Mohammed V. The grandfather of the current king, Mohammed V is part of the Alawite dynasty that claims descent from the Prophet Muhammad. He was thrust onto the political scene at a turbulent time in Morocco's history when the French named him sultan in 1927. He was a man who straddled two worlds, speaking French as well as Arabic, and working with French as well as Moroccan leaders. He supported and assisted the Moroccan movement toward independence even while the French pressured him to remain loyal to Morocco's French rulers. While the Germans were in control of Morocco, he resisted their orders and offered protection to Jewish people whose families had lived in Morocco for centuries. He guided the nation through the dramatic political changes that led to independence in 1956. He only enjoyed five years as leader of independent Morocco, dying suddenly after surgery in 1961.

Control in the South

Although Morocco had become independent, Spain still controlled some territories in the region. Along the Mediterranean coast, it held the cities of Ceuta and Melilla. It also held the regions of Tarfaya and Ifni along the Atlantic coast. Spain gave up Tarfaya in 1958 and Ifni in 1970, in part hoping to keep control of its Mediterranean cities.

Spain also held a wide swath of desert called the Spanish Sahara. Well after Morocco gained independence in 1956, this vast territory remained in Spanish hands. Morocco,

Honoring a Saharan Leader

In Morocco's most isolated regions, people have often looked to local rulers such as tribal chiefs for guidance. In the Sahara, such leaders frequently move across vast swaths of desert by camel. Sheik Mohammed Laghdaf was such a leader. He inspired the Sahrawi people to resist both the French and Spanish who occupied their territories. When he died in 1960, after decades of leading the resistance to colonial rule in the Sahara, he was buried at Tan-Tan, in southern Morocco. His tomb is now the center of a religious festival known as the Tan Tan Moussem, held in his honor in December each year.

During this festival, nomadic people arrive on their camels from distant Saharan regions to join in a celebration of their traditions and culture. Dozens of nomadic groups come together for this annual festival, and as many as eight hundred tents are set up in the desert. Camel trading goes on throughout the *moussem*. People also enjoy traditional singing, dancing, and storytelling, and catching up on family news. Through all of this, they honor Mohammed Laghdaf.

however, claimed the territory as its own, and local nomadic groups began fighting Spanish control.

In 1975, the International Court of Justice declared that Morocco's ties to Amazigh groups in the Spanish Sahara, also known as the Western Sahara, were not strong enough to allow Morocco to claim the region as part of its territory. The response from King Hassan II was swift. To secure Morocco's claim over the Spanish Sahara, King Hassan II announced that a peaceful army of 350,000 men and women would embark on a march into the territory. He called it the Green March, because the color green is a symbol of Islam. The marchers

During the Green March, Moroccans entered Spanish Sahara with Moroccan national flags held high.

would be armed only with the Qur'an, the holy book of Islam, and faith in their mission. The march began on November 6, 1975, at Tarfaya. Accompanied by the heavily armed Moroccan army, the marchers crossed the border, making their claim on the territory.

Within a week, Spain gave up its claims to the region, which it had held since 1884. In the following years, Morocco strengthened its physical grip on the region by building a massive sand and rock wall separating the part of Western Sahara controlled by Morocco from the rest of the territory, which is controlled by a group of local nomadic people calling themselves

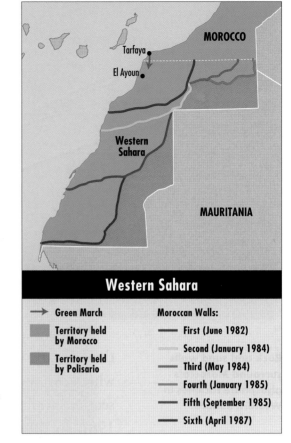

Western Sahara

→ Green March

▢ Territory held by Morocco

▢ Territory held by Polisario

Moroccan Walls:
— First (June 1982)
— Second (January 1984)
— Third (May 1984)
— Fourth (January 1985)
— Fifth (September 1985)
— Sixth (April 1987)

Hassan II was king of Morocco for thirty-eight years.

Ancient Land, Modern Nation **53**

for work. Throughout North Africa, the population is overwhelmingly young, but many of the young people have little hope of finding a job or making a better life for themselves.

The protests, which became known as the Arab Spring, spread to other North African countries, including Libya and Egypt. In February 2011, protests also began in Morocco. Young people demonstrated in cities and towns throughout the nation. Instead of cracking down on the tens of thousands of people who filled the streets and public squares, as authori-

In recent years, many Moroccans have taken part in demonstrations in support of greater rights for women.

ties had in other countries, Mohammed VI took a different approach. In a live television appearance on March 9, 2011, he announced a new constitution. This surprised Moroccans, who did not expect a positive reaction from the king, and the most robust protests quickly cooled down.

The new constitution promised to reduce the king's power and give more power to elected members of the government. But some people complained that the new constitution did little to change how Morocco is governed. For example, under the new constitution, the prime minister is appointed by the king. Other people, however, are optimistic that political and economic reform are possible as Moroccans gain more say in their own government.

As Morocco makes political and economic reforms, cities such as Casablanca are thriving.

Ancient Land, Modern Nation **57**

CHAPTER 5

Ruling the Kingdom

THE KINGDOM OF MOROCCO IS A CONSTITUTIONAL monarchy. This means it is ruled by a king who inherited the title but who must follow the laws contained in a constitution. Morocco's current constitution was written in 2011 by an eighteen-member committee, all appointed by the king. The constitution gives the king wide-ranging power but does allow for political parties and an elected parliament. The king, however, can dismiss the parliament if he disagrees with its decisions. The king also appoints the prime minister who oversees the day-to-day operations of the government. Although Morocco has democratic institutions, all of them are under the control of the king.

Opposite: **King Mohammed VI has wide-ranging power. He is the political, military, and religious leader of the country.**

The flag of Morocco consists of a field of bright red with a green five-pointed star in the middle. The flag was adopted as the symbol of Morocco in 1915, before it became an independent nation. The green five-pointed star is associated with Islam. Green is also said to represent the green of the palm tree, a vital tree in the desert. Red represents royalty and symbolizes bravery and strength.

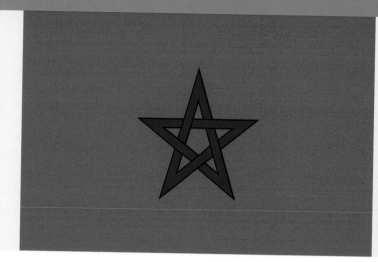

The King of Morocco

Mohammed VI became king of Morocco when his father, King Hassan II, died in 1999. July 30, the day he officially took the throne, is a public holiday in Morocco. Mohammed was the heir apparent (the expected ruler) from the time of his birth and was groomed to take over from his father. Along with his grandfather Mohammed V, the current king is part

Mohammed was groomed to be king from the time he was a young boy. At age ten, he attended a memorial service for the president of France.

Mohammed VI waves to the crowd on the day of the bay'a ceremony. On this day, Moroccans pledge their loyalty to the king.

of the Alawite family that has ruled Morocco since the mid-seventeenth century, including largely ceremonial leadership during the colonial period. Moreover, the Alawite family claims direct descent from the Prophet Muhammad, who founded the religion of Islam. This connection gives the Alawite kings of Morocco a unique position of spiritual as well as political power. For example, the new constitution forbids Moroccans from criticizing the king. If a person simply reports that there was a protest against the monarchy, he or she can be arrested.

Each year, Mohammed VI receives an oath of loyalty from the Moroccan people in a ritual ceremony known as the bay'a. For many Moroccans, including ministers who participate and ordinary citizens who watch the ceremony on

The code included many significant changes: The minimum legal age for marriage was raised to eighteen, for both men and women. The new code gives women more say in marriage contracts and makes men and women equal partners in the marriage. Women have the first right to custody of children in the event of a divorce. Additionally, if a woman does have custody of the children, she may remain in the marital home. Previously, a man could simply say, "I divorce you" and turn his wife out of the house, leaving her to live on the streets.

A woman and her children in Fès.

A Look at the Capital

Rabat, the capital of Morocco since independence, is located on the country's Atlantic coast. The area was a great trading center during the time of the Phoenicians and the Romans, more than 2,500 years ago. The name Rabat comes from the Arabic word *ribat*, a fortress or stronghold. The Almohad dynasty built massive walls to fortify the site in the twelfth century. The city's prime location on the ocean made it a target for pirates who attacked ships arriving in the port.

Rabat stands just across the Bou Regreg River from the ancient city of Salé. The two cities are connected by the Hassan II Bridge, which was completed in 2011. It replaced an old bridge that was no longer able to handle the enormous increase in traffic in this rapidly growing metropolitan area. The two cities form one large metropolitan area with a population of more than 2.5 million people. Rabat proper has a population of about 1,656,000.

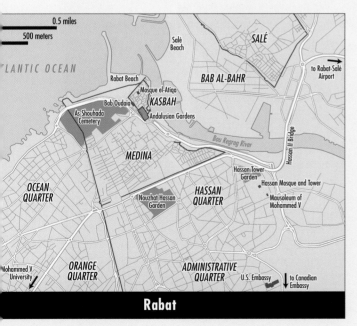

Rabat

When the French established a protectorate over Morocco in 1912, they chose Rabat as their headquarters. At the time, the city consisted mainly of the walled old city, or medina. In the century since, Rabat has expanded with modern roads, transportation links, and extensive gardens. Some of the oldest structures in the city include Bab Oudaia, the twelfth-century gate to the fortress. The Mosque el-Atiqa, also built in the twelfth century, is the oldest mosque in the city. Reminders of French occupation are found everywhere, including at the beautiful Andalusian Gardens, which were laid out by the French. The Mausoleum of Mohammed V is located east of the medina. It contains the tombs of Hassan II and Mohammed V, the current king's father and grandfather, respectively.

Not everyone in Morocco agrees with this new code. Some believe it takes away rights that are basic to Muslim life. Moreover, enacting a law does not mean that everyone is following it. Many people say it will take at least a generation for the law to fully take effect. Currently, it remains easy for a father to go before a judge and ask for permission to marry off his daughter while she is still a minor. It is estimated that the judges give this permission in 90 percent of the cases. And the inheritance law has not changed, even on paper. Males still inherit twice as much as females, by law.

Bassima Hakkaoui became the minister for solidarity, women, family, and social development in 2012. She is the only female cabinet member in Morocco.

The National Anthem

The Cherifian Anthem has been the anthem of Morocco since before it became independent. The music was written by Léo Morgan in 1956, and a new set of lyrics was added by Ali Sqalli Houssaini in 1970.

Transliterated Arabic lyrics

Manbita al-ahrar

Mashriqa al-anwar

Muntada as-su'dadi wa- imah

Dumta muntadah wa- imah

'Ishta fi il-awtan

Lil-'ula 'unwan

Mil'a kulli janan

Dhikra kulli lisan

Bir-ru i, bil-jasadi

Habba fatak labba nidak

Fi fami wa-fi dami

Hawaka thara nur wa-nar

Ikhwati hayya lil-'ula sa'ya

Nushhidi id-dunya anna huna na ya

Bi-shi'ar

Allah, al-wa an, al-malik

English translation

Root of the free,

Rising place of the lights,

Forum of glory and its protector,

May you perpetuate as its forum and its protector.

May you live among the homelands

As an address for grandeur

Filling every garden

conveyed by every tongue.

With the spirit, with the body,

Your son has come to answer your call.

In my mouth and in my blood,

Your love stirred up as light and fire.

Let's go brothers! Heading for grandeur,

Making the world witness that we here perpetually live

With the motto:

God, homeland, king.

CHAPTER 6

On the Job

MOROCCO'S ECONOMY IS DEPENDENT ON A FEW major industries, including tourism, farming, and mining. Tourism brings more foreign money into the country than any other industry. But there is an even larger source of foreign money in Morocco: money sent home by Moroccans living abroad. Most Moroccans who leave the country in search of work head to the French-speaking nations of France and Belgium. About 1.9 million Moroccans live in France, where they make up 2 percent of the total population. Moroccans living abroad usually maintain close ties to their families in Morocco and send money home on a regular basis. The Moroccan economy depends on these remittances, as they are called. It is estimated that in recent years Moroccans have sent $5.6 billion home to relatives in Morocco each year. One of Morocco's biggest exports is its hard-working population.

Opposite: **A man sells food at a stall in Marrakech.**

Tourism

Morocco's government has invested heavily in tourism in recent years. Morocco has a unique combination of ancient cities and dramatic landscapes, and its location, close to Europe, ensures a steady flow of visitors. Many people visit the medinas of Morocco's cities. These are the oldest part of the cities, usually walled in for protection. They are filled with mazelike alleyways and large souks, or markets, where local

Tourists shop for fabrics in Fès. The narrow lanes of the medina draw visitors from around the world.

In the Medina

At the heart of Marrakech lies the public square called Djemma el-Fna. This square teems with shoppers, food, musicians, and tourists. Henna artists use a temporary dye to create decorative art on the skin of local women preparing for weddings and on tourists looking for a temporary tattoo and a taste of Moroccan culture. Hundreds of tiny shops are crowded into souks, or marketplaces. A shopper looking for a rug to buy may be invited to enjoy a glass of mint tea while the shop owner rolls out dozens of rugs for consideration.

At night, food vendors bring out stacks of cooking stoves and grills, supports for their stalls, and lights.

Each vendor heads for a numbered space on the square. The vendors set up their kitchens and get ready to serve a steady stream of hungry people. Steam rises from a hundred different stalls where traditional Moroccan dishes are prepared.

Much less pleasant smells drift from the tanneries of Marrakech (above). These are steaming, open-air pots where leather is prepared and dyed to make the handbags and luggage found in the souks. The smell is dreadful and there's little room to walk between the pots, but many visitors make their way to the tanneries to see where some of Morocco's handmade goods get their start.

Moroccan craftspeople make pottery that is used in many hotels and restaurants.

people and visitors alike shop for food, clothing, and household goods. Many of the souks have stalls where visitors can watch craftspeople make the items they sell.

Tourism is a major part of the Moroccan economy, accounting for about 9 percent of all the money earned in the country. It employs about eight hundred thousand people directly in businesses such as hotels, tour companies, beach resorts, and transportation. Waiters, chefs, drivers, guides, and interpreters all find work in the tourism industry. It is estimated that another five indirect jobs are created for every direct job in tourism. People employed indirectly by tourism include people who make crafts and provide food or entertainment. Other people whose jobs are indirectly the result of tourism are the architects who design hotels and the construction workers who build them; the weavers who make the rugs, bedding, and tapestries for hotel rooms; and the potters who make the dishes.

Morocco hosts about ten million foreign visitors a year, and that number is growing. About three million of the visitors come from France and another one and a half million from Spain. Both of those countries have cultural ties to Morocco and are located close by, just across the Mediterranean Sea. Only about 2 percent of the visitors to Morocco are from the

Beaches such as those at Al Hoceima, on the Mediterranean coast, attract thousands of tourists every year.

United States. Many American visitors are drawn to Morocco for its rich culture, intriguing architecture, and excellent food. Europeans are more likely to travel to Morocco's beaches.

As the number of tourists increases, more people are venturing beyond the traditional destinations of Marrakech, Fès, and Meknès. This increases the jobs available to young people in different areas across the country. Ecotourism and adventure tourism are also on the rise. Surfers flock to Morocco's Atlantic beaches, where the waves are dramatic and dependable. Windsurfing appeals to those willing to let the air take them skimming along the water.

Agriculture

In spite of its arid climate, agriculture employs about 40 percent of Morocco's total workforce. Most people who work in agriculture are farmers with small land holdings. Morocco has an estimated 1,500,000 small farms. The farmers produce little more than they need to sustain themselves.

About three-quarters of Morocco's total land area is not suitable for farming because it is too dry. Farmers irrigate much of the land that is suitable for farming. They capture the rain that does fall and then use it carefully.

Roughly 80 percent of the crops grown in Morocco are cereals such as barley, wheat, and corn. Potatoes, olives, oranges, apples, fava beans, chickpeas, lentils, and peas are also grown.

Men sort recently harvested dates. Some date palm trees produce as much as 300 pounds (130 kg) of dates a year.

Delicious Dates

Dates, which grow on date palm trees, are a major crop in Morocco. Most of the country's dates are grown on small plots of land by individual farmers. The palm trees flourish in the hot, dry climate of the south. The Draa Valley in southern Morocco is a major center of date growing.

There are dozens of species of dates, but the most prized is the Medjool date. The Medjool is difficult to grow because it is extremely sensitive to the air quality and the amount of moisture in the soil. It was once reserved only for royalty and is typically more expensive than other types of dates. The less expensive Deglet Noor date is believed to have originated in Algeria. It is widely used in cooking in Morocco and is also an important export crop. A third popular type is the Halawi date. Its high sugar content makes it very sweet, and it is often offered as a dessert in Moroccan homes.

Some Moroccans also keep livestock. The most common farm animal is sheep, which number about nineteen million. Moroccans also raise cattle and goats. Animals such as these provide leather, wool, and skins to craft industries. In addition, many Moroccans also keep beasts of burden such as camels, mules, horses, and donkeys to help carry goods.

Fishing

Although Morocco has a long coastline, the nation's fishing industry is not large. Small-scale fishers working the rich waters off the country's west coast carry out much of the fishing. These fishing grounds, where sardines, bonito, and tuna swim, are known as the Canary Current because they face the Canary Islands, Spanish islands off the coast of Africa. Morocco's fishers do not have access to good harbor facilities and plants to process fish, so the nation's fishing industry has lagged behind that of other nations. In order to earn revenue from the fishing grounds, Morocco rents its waters to foreign fishing vessels from the European Union. The waters off Morocco have been overfished, so the number of boats allowed to fish off Morocco's coast is limited in order to allow the fish population to rebound.

A fisher carries tuna he caught near Taghazout, in southern Morocco. About one hundred thousand people make their living fishing in Morocco.

The dirham is the basic unit of currency in Morocco. It is divided into one hundred centimes. Paper bills come in denominations of 20, 50, 100, and 200 dirhams. Coins come in values of 1, 2, 5, and 10 dirhams. There are also 5, 10, 20, and 50 centime coins. In 2014, 1 dirham equaled about 11 U.S. cents.

King Mohammed VI appears on the front of all paper bills. On the back are images of places or scenes typical of Morocco. For example, the 100-dirham note depicts men riding camels across a desert, while the 200-dirham note shows the lighthouse and port in Tangier.

Manufacturing

Manufacturing plays a small but growing role in the Moroccan economy. Food processing makes up a large part of the manufacturing sector. Workers mill flour, refine sugar, and can fruits and vegetables. Chemical products, bricks, ceramics, textiles, iron, and steel are also made in Morocco.

Morocco also has a significant automobile manufacturing industry. In 2012, a massive automobile factory opened in Melloussa, a suburb of Tangier. The plant makes Renault cars, a popular French brand, and employs three thousand people. This plant is designed to make basic, low-cost cars for people in less wealthy countries. These cars do not compete with the more expensive cars produced in Europe. Within a year of opening, the capacity of the plant was increased, so it was producing 340,000 vehicles a year. Renault also builds cars at a factory in Casablanca.

What Morocco Grows, Makes, and Mines

AGRICULTURE (2012)

Wheat	3,878,000 metric tons
Olives	1,315,790 metric tons
Barley	1,201,390 metric tons

MANUFACTURING (VALUE ADDED, 2010)

Chemical products	US$2,040,000,000
Food products	US$1,818,000,000
Bricks, cement, and ceramics	US$1,523,000,000

MINING (2012)

Phosphate rock	28,000,000 metric tons
Barite	800,000 metric tons
Zinc	46,000 metric tons

Mining

Phosphate mining plays a large role in Morocco's economy. Phosphates, as both raw ore and as manufactured products, are the country's most valuable export. Phosphate is a vital ingredient in the production of fertilizer for agriculture. Morocco possesses 75 percent of the world's phosphate reserves and is the third-largest producer of phosphates in the world. While China and the United States are bigger producers, they keep most of the production for their own use. Much of the rest of the world depends on Morocco's phosphates. Morocco's main phosphate mine is Boucraa in the Sahara. This desolate place is far from the port where the goods are shipped out. A remarkable

93-mile-long (150 km) conveyor belt carries the phosphates to the port of El Ayoun. The belt, raised high on supports, snakes across the desert, following the ups and downs of the landscape.

Moroccans have also found other ways to easily transport the phosphate ore to ports. A pipeline transports phosphate slurry, a thick soup made from mixing phosphate rock and water, from mines at Khouribga to the port of Jorf Lasfar. This has eliminated the need for trains. Since Khouribga is 2,789 feet (850 m) above sea level, the entire pipeline runs downhill. This allows gravity to do much of the work of moving the slurry along.

The mine is part of OCP, the official state agency in charge of phosphates. OCP mines 28 million metric tons of phosphate

A phosphate factory near El Jadida, along the coast. An estimated 50 billion metric tons of phosphates lie underground in Morocco and Western Sahara.

rock a year, yielding 4.5 million tons of phosphate fertilizer. The ore is taken from open-pit mines, which create many environmental challenges. The main phosphate mine is located in the Sahara. As the wind blows across the empty land, it picks up loose dust produced by the mining operation, polluting the atmosphere.

Other minerals found in Morocco include coal, iron ore, and zinc. Morocco is one of the world's largest producers of barite, which is used in oil drilling and in the production of some paints and plastics.

Energy

In recent years, Morocco has gotten much of its electricity from burning

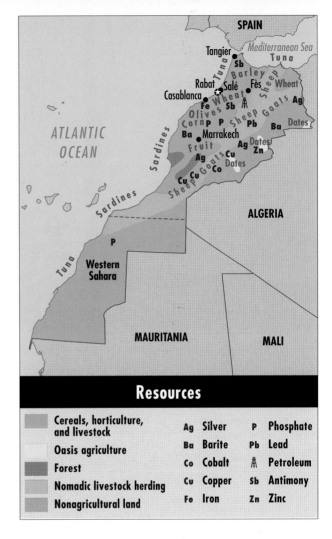

Resources

Cereals, horticulture, and livestock	Ag	Silver	P	Phosphate
Oasis agriculture	Ba	Barite	Pb	Lead
Forest	Co	Cobalt	⚒	Petroleum
Nomadic livestock herding	Cu	Copper	Sb	Antimony
Nonagricultural land	Fe	Iron	Zn	Zinc

coal. But as Morocco's energy needs are increasing, the nation has been looking toward other sources of energy.

With its abundant sunshine, Morocco can produce a tremendous amount of solar energy. Much of the nation enjoys 3,000 hours of sunshine a year while the Sahara basks in up to 3,600 hours of sun a year. Unlike coal or oil, sunshine is renewable, meaning there is an endless supply of it. Solar energy also has the advantage of not polluting the environment. Many Moroccan homes have solar panels that heat

People gather for the opening of a wind farm in Melloussa, near Tangier. It is one of the largest wind farms in Morocco.

water for washing and cooking, and large solar energy power plants are now being constructed. It is estimated that by the year 2020, solar energy will produce about 14 percent of all the power used in Morocco.

Wind is another renewable energy source used in Morocco. With the fierce Atlantic Ocean winds blowing from the west, Morocco is well situated to make use of wind energy. Hundreds of wind turbines have been set up along the coast, some on the land and others offshore.

Transportation

Morocco has an extensive highway and rail system that makes it easy to travel between major cities. The nation's major airport, Mohammed V International Airport, is near Casablanca, but many other airports also provide service to Europe.

Since King Mohammed VI came to power, he has made expanding the nation's ports a priority. This has brought in much more cargo and made Morocco an important export and tourist link to Europe. More traffic at the ports means much more employment. It takes many people to design or build a new port or expand an old one. Once the port is up and running, many workers are needed to handle the ships, cargo, and passengers.

Morocco's busiest ports are in the northern part of the country. One of the biggest projects of recent years was the creation of Tanger Med, a port 24 miles (40 km) east of the city of Tangier. The location of the port, at the Strait of Gibraltar, just 9 miles (15 km) from Europe, creates easy access to a market with hundreds of millions of consumers. A second port, Tanger Med II, was soon added. The port in Casablanca has also grown in recent years. A new terminal opened at the port in 2010, greatly expanding the port's capacity to handle newly manufactured automobiles.

Cranes load giant containers onto a ship at Tanger Med 1.

CHAPTER 7

People and Languages

MORE THAN THIRTY-THREE MILLION PEOPLE live in Morocco, but they are not spread evenly throughout the country. The Atlas Mountains form a natural barrier between the north and south. Most of the population is found in the more temperate north and along the coast rather than in the hotter and drier regions farther south. Morocco's major cities are located in these regions. In recent years, people have been moving into the cities from the countryside, looking for work. Today, About 58 percent of the people now live in urban areas.

About 20 percent of the people live in the Atlas or Rif Mountains. Most people in these areas belong to Amazigh groups. Small numbers of people also live in oases in the Sahara.

Morocco's Many Cultures

The Amazigh peoples were the original inhabitants of the Maghreb, a region that includes all of North Africa, west of Egypt. They lived there long before the Arab people came

Opposite: **People fill the streets of Marrakech. The city has experienced dramatic population growth in recent years, with the number of residents almost tripling between 1971 and 2010.**

Population of Major Cities (2014 est.)	
Casablanca	3,145,000
Rabat	1,656,000
Fès	965,000
Salé	903,000
Marrakech	839,000

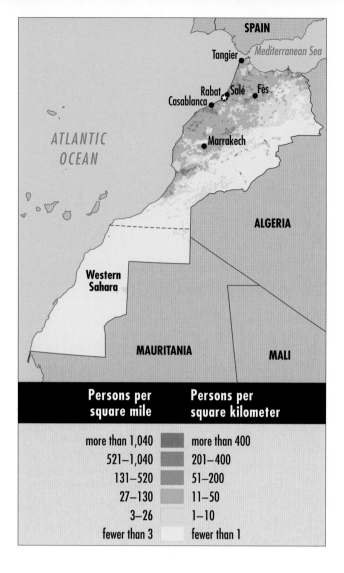

Persons per square mile		Persons per square kilometer
more than 1,040		more than 400
521–1,040		201–400
131–520		51–200
27–130		11–50
3–26		1–10
fewer than 3		fewer than 1

Ethnic Morocco

Arab-Amazigh	99%
Other	1%

from the east and conquered the area. *Maghreb* is an Arabic word that refers to the west, its geographical location in Africa and its status as the westernmost part of the territories that were converted to Islam in the seventh century. The Arabs brought their language, their culture, and their new religion, Islam, to Maghreb.

The Amazigh peoples were at a disadvantage in their battles against the Arabs because they did not have leaders who ruled large areas, so the different Amazigh groups did not always work together. Instead, each Amazigh village had its own leader and belief system. When the Arabs conquered the region, the Amazigh peoples added Islam to their beliefs. In many places, the Arab and Amazigh populations merged, but Amazigh language and culture continued to survive in isolated areas, particularly in the mountains. Today, Amazigh people account for 30 to 40 percent of Morocco's total population. However, almost all Moroccans have some Amazigh ancestry. People of European descent make up about 1 percent of the population.

Other ethnic groups arrived in North Africa from across the Mediterranean Sea. Some were fleeing persecution in their own countries, while others were working to expand the territory or influence of their own nation. Both Spain and France colonized the region, contributing to the mix of cultures, languages, architecture, food, and political systems. The French language, in particular, took hold in Morocco, thanks largely to the government organization the French brought with them. Moroccans who learned the French language had more job opportunities. Likewise, with Spanish rule in place in some coastal regions on both the Atlantic and the Mediterranean, the culture and language of Spain were added to the mix.

Amazigh women with their children. Some Amazigh women have geometric tattoos on their faces.

This layering of cultures, languages, and belief systems gave Morocco a unique multilingual population. Because of Morocco's diverse population and history, plus its location on the edge of Africa, within easy reach of Europe, Morocco has been a country that many outsiders feel at home in.

Language

Morocco's rich tapestry of cultures is reflected in the languages used in the country. Arabic is the most common language spoken in Morocco. In the past, the country's Arab rulers had tried to stamp out Amazigh culture, going so far as to ban Amazigh languages. For a time, the Amazigh languages went underground, but now they have resurfaced and are used with pride. In 2011, Tamazight, an Amazigh language, became one of Morocco's two official languages, along with Arabic. About 40 percent of the Moroccan population speaks an Amazigh language as their first language. Many Amazigh people also speak Arabic, but people in more rural and isolated areas usually speak only an Amazigh language.

French is widely spoken in Morocco. This is a legacy of Morocco's former status as a protectorate of France as well as the two nations' ongoing economic and cultural ties. Being able to speak French is crucial for anyone entering government service, as French is widely used in business and government, and official documents are translated into French. Both French and English are taught in Moroccan schools, and both are used widely throughout Africa. A small minority of Moroccans speaks Spanish as a second language.

The Arabic and Amazigh languages use different alphabets. The Arabic alphabet includes twenty-eight letters, most of which are made of curving lines. Dots are sometimes incorporated as well. There are no capitals in Arabic, but the letters are written differently depending on whether they appear at the beginning, middle, or end of a word, or stand alone.

French is taught in schools throughout Morocco.

Common Arabic Phrases

lla	no
iyyeh, n'am	yes
afak	please
shokran	thank you
salam	hello, peace
bslama	good-bye
wakha	okay
daba	now

Arabic writing features flowing lines and is often used to decorate buildings.

Amazigh languages can be written using different alphabets. Many writers and publications prefer to use the Berber Latin alphabet. This alphabet is similar to the alphabet used

Amazigh languages can be written using many different alphabets. Here, each row of red letters immediately below a row of blue letters is in Neo-Tifinagh.

in English, but it has thirty-four letters rather than twenty-six. It does not use the *o*, *p*, and *v* but does include eleven letters that are modified versions of other letters such as an *r* with a dot underneath. Other writers use Arabic when writing Amazigh languages. Since 2003, some schools in Morocco have been using Neo-Tifinagh, a modern version of an old alphabet used for Amazigh languages.

In Morocco, young children attend school for about five and a half hours a day.

Education

Primary school in Morocco starts at age six or seven and lasts for six years. About half the students go on to secondary education, which is divided into three years of middle school and three years of high school. Young people who complete their

The Oldest University

Many people argue that the world's oldest university is Qarawiyin University, which was established in 859 in Fès. It began as a madrassa, a Muslim school that is part of a mosque. Both the school and the mosque were founded by Fatima al-Fihri, the well-educated daughter of a wealthy merchant. After its founding, Qarawiyin quickly became a major educational center in the Muslim world. Scholars from around North Africa and beyond came to teach or study there. In the twentieth century, Qarawiyin University became part of Morocco's state educational system.

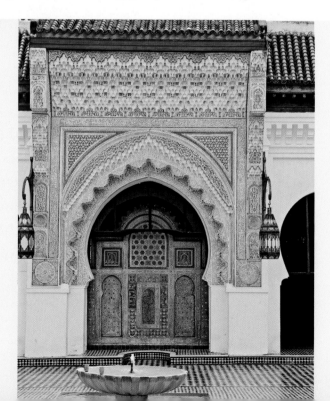

secondary education can continue their education at a university. Morocco is home to fourteen universities and many other institutes of higher education. The largest is Mohammed V University in Rabat. Because jobs are scarce in Morocco, many of the most highly educated Moroccans immigrate to Europe, where job opportunities are greater.

Although all Moroccan children are legally required to attend school until age thirteen, in practice, many children do not attend school because their families need them to work. This is especially common in rural areas and among girls.

Mohammed V University at Souissi has started a mentoring program that advises female students on moving into the professional world.

In addition, the education of some children is limited because of the languages they speak. As Morocco changed from a French protectorate to an independent nation, it introduced Arabic as the language of instruction schools. Math and science, however, continued to be taught in French. By 1989, enough Arabic-speaking teachers had been trained that French was no longer used in elementary or secondary school. French remains the language of instruction at the university level.

About two out of every three Moroccan adults can read and write. Women have a lower literacy rate than men, because many women either never attended school or were pressured to drop out early.

Women in Tioute, in southern Morocco, attend a class to learn to read and write.

Although one of the goals in Moroccan education is for students to become fluent in Arabic in primary school, this poses a problem for children in predominantly Amazigh areas. Many of these children start first grade without knowing any Arabic. Since Tamazight has now joined Arabic as one of Morocco's official languages, the students can be taught Tamazight in primary school before learning Arabic as they move on to middle and high school. But many students drop out after primary school, and they will likely not have another chance to learn Arabic.

Today, with the use of the Internet growing rapidly, English has become the most important international language. Moroccans begin studying English in middle school. Many young adults who did not have the opportunity to learn English in school take classes to learn English or improve their language skills.

Students in Casablanca work together on a project to redevelop buildings that are no longer used.

CHAPTER 8

Life of the Spirit

ISLAM IS THE OFFICIAL RELIGION OF MOROCCO, AND it is followed by about 99 percent of the population. Morocco guarantees the right to freedom of religion, however, and some people choose other religions. About one hundred thousand people in Morocco, most of them of French descent, are Christian. Another five thousand Moroccans are Jewish. Morocco's Jewish population was once more than two hundred thousand, but most Moroccan Jews emigrated to Israel, Europe, or North America in the twentieth century. The country's Jewish population is expected to decline further in the coming years as the Jewish people now living in Morocco are growing old, and younger Jews have moved out of the country.

Opposite: **A man in Fès ritually purifies himself before entering a mosque to pray. This practice is called *wudu*.**

The Origins of Islam

The religion Islam arose in what is now Mecca, Saudi Arabia, in the seventh century CE with the teachings of the Prophet

Studying the Qur'an

The Qur'an, the holy book of Islam, offers guidance to people in their daily lives and touches on issues of religious law. To study the Qur'an, many students go to a religious school called a madrassa. Some madrassas in Morocco are famous for their history as well as their architecture. The Madrassa Ben Youssef in Marrakech was founded in the fourteenth century. Students lived in tiny rooms at the madrassa, where they spent many hours studying and memorizing the Qur'an. Students also studied Islamic law and science. This madrassa is no longer a school and is now open to the public. Visitors can admire the building's beautiful geometric designs and calligraphy, which reproduces phrases from the Qur'an.

A man reading the Qur'an in Morocco

The Madrassa Bou Inania is one of the most beautiful and elaborately decorated buildings in Fès.

The Madrassa Bou Inania, in Fès, was also built in the fourteenth century. As in many religious buildings in Morocco, the courtyard includes a place for people to wash their faces, legs, and hands before prayer. Non-Muslims may enter the madrassa to see the architecture and to enjoy the peace and quiet just steps away from the busy, noisy streets.

Interpreting the Qur'an

The Qur'an touches on a wide variety of issues, but the interpretations of the statements in the Qur'an can vary tremendously. For example, the Qur'an states that people should dress modestly. This has been interpreted in many different ways, so some Muslim women dress in the same manner as people of other religions. Other people have interpreted modest dress to mean that women should cover their hair, arms, and legs. Still others have argued that women should cover their entire bodies with a loose garment and cover their faces as well. In Morocco, many women wear headscarves, and many older women cover their bodies completely.

CHAPTER 9

Arts and Sports

MOROCCO HAS A LONG TRADITION OF EXQUISITE crafts. The alleys of its souks are lined with painted pots, glass lamps, carved wood, leather handbags, silver jewelry, and copper teapots. Not to be missed are the rugs. Rugmaking is one of Morocco's oldest and proudest traditions.

Handmade Moroccan rugs have a history going back thousands of years. They vary in style, colors, and patterns according to the needs of the people who make and use them. In the cold Atlas Mountains, heavy-pile rugs help keep out the bitter winter winds. In the desert regions, lightweight rugs help to block the harsh rays of the sun and protect people from windblown sand. Rugs serve as saddle blankets on camels and horses. They are used as wall coverings, sleeping mats, and bedcovers. In Moroccan homes it is traditional to cover the floors with rugs—often four or five in the room. The patterns and colors

Opposite: **Rugs hang in a market in Fès. Each region of Morocco has its own distinctive rug pattern.**

Music

Moroccan music has been influenced by the music of Amazigh and Arab peoples and also contains strains of African and Spanish music. Amazigh folk music is popular and often includes drums, flutes, lutes, and rhythmic hand clapping. Some traditional Moroccan musicians such as the Master

A street musician in Marrakech plays a simple string instrument called a *ginbri*.

Musicians of Jajouka create trancelike music. Hailing from the Rif Mountains, they have become world-renowned. They have performed with jazz musicians such as Ornette Coleman and rock groups such as the Rolling Stones.

Many forms of Moroccan music blend folk traditions with popular music. Chaabi is often performed at celebrations. It combines songs of love with violin music, and more recently, electronic keyboards. Rai music mixes traditional and Western music and has lyrics that often deal with social and political issues. Moroccan hip-hop stars, such as a performer named Muslim, also sing frequently about social problems.

Moroccan children play soccer wherever they can find space. Here, boys play in the old town of Marrakech.

Sporting Life

Soccer is by far the most popular sport in Morocco, as it is throughout most of the world. Morocco's national team takes part in the World Cup every four years, along with numerous other national soccer teams. This tournament is the most popular sporting event in the world.

Pioneering Athlete

When Nawal El Moutawakel raced across the finish line to win the women's 400-meter hurdles event at the 1984 Summer Olympics, she made history in several ways. She became the first Moroccan woman to win an Olympic medal of any kind. She also became the first African woman and the first Muslim woman to take home a gold medal from the Olympics.

El Moutawakel became an advocate for women's sports in Morocco and created a 5-kilometer run for women in Casablanca. The race has grown in popularity and now attracts up to thirty thousand participants. El Moutawakel has served as the minister of sport in Morocco and is now a member of the International Olympic Committee. She presided over the committee that selected the cities to host the 2012 and 2016 games.

Morocco also takes part in the Summer Olympic Games, where Moroccan athletes have won medals in many different track events and in boxing. At the 2012 Summer Olympics, Abdalaati Iguider took a bronze medal in the 1,500-meter race. Many Moroccans have participated in skiing events in the Winter Olympics, though they have not yet won any medals.

To the Limit

One of the most grueling running races ever created is the Marathon des Sables, or Marathon of the Sands. This race is much more than a marathon. In fact, it is the equivalent of six marathons, a total of about 150 miles (240 km), run over five or six days, depending on the route. This kind of extreme race is known as an ultramarathon. It takes place entirely in the Sahara of southern Morocco, where the temperature is usually more than 100°F (38°C). The runners encounter many kinds of challenging terrain as they make their way

across the Sahara: sand dunes, mountains, and roads pitted with small rocks and pebbles. The task is all the more daunting because the runners must carry all their food, sleeping gear, and other supplies on their backs.

The first Marathon des Sables took place in 1986. Considered by many to be the toughest race on earth, the race attracts more and more entrants each year, but the number of competitors is capped at about one thousand people. In 2014, the men's winner was Moroccan Rachid El Morabity, while American Nikki Kimball won among women.

Daily Life

FAMILY IS AT THE CENTER OF LIFE IN MOROCCO. FAMILY members spend a great deal of time together, and the needs of the family are put ahead of the needs of the individual. Extended families live together, so elderly parents live with their married children. In Morocco, people show great respect for their elders.

Morocco's population is relatively young. Families have an average of two or three children, and many adults have moved to Europe to look for work. Today, more than one in four Moroccans is age fifteen or younger. Moroccans live an average of seventy-six years.

Opposite: **A young man in the Sahara wears a *djellaba*, a traditional Amazigh robe. The djellaba keeps the sun and sand off the skin during the day and provides warmth at night.**

Young and Old	
Age Group	Percent of population
Up to age 15	27%
16–24	18%
25–54	42%
55–64	7%
65 and older	6%

During the wedding ceremony, the bride is carried around the room on a large chair.

Wedding Traditions

The occasion of a marriage is marked by several days of parties and lavish meals. The families of both the bride and the groom host parties for the guests, so many guests end up traveling back and forth between the two homes. Men and women usually celebrate separately, so in each home there is a women's party and a men's party. In very traditional Muslim families, the bride is secluded during most of the celebration, unseen by the guests and by her husband-to-be. She instead spends time with her female relatives.

The female guests dress up in their finest clothes and wear a marriage belt, an elaborately embroidered stiff circle of leather.

Charge!

Fantasia is one of the most awe-inspiring events in Morocco. Traditionally, it was performed at Amazigh weddings. At the fantasia, riders on horses, dressed in traditional outfits, are spread out in a row. The riders urge their animals to race as fast as they can toward the audience. Just when it seems they will mow everyone down, the riders bring the horses to an abrupt stop while at the same time firing old muskets or rifles into the air. This requires that the participants be accomplished riders and shooters and that the horses be perfectly trained. While the charge of the horses seems chaotic, it is carefully orchestrated. These performances often take place during religious festivals called *moussems*.

When women arrive for a wedding party, they are dressed in a loose caftan that covers them from head to toe. When they enter the home of the bride or groom, they peel off the caftans revealing colorful floor-length dresses.

Meanwhile, behind closed doors, the bride is being prepared for her brief appearance at the wedding. Special wedding clothes, jewelry, and a headdress are rented for the occasion. Women called Neggafates arrive to help the bride put on this once-in-a-lifetime outfit. She then sits on a special platform called the *ammariya* and is danced around the room on others' shoulders. After this, the bride disappears again for the rest of the ceremony.

Music and dancing are an important part of the wedding ceremony. The dancing, eating, and celebrating goes on all

Music is a vital part of every festival in Morocco.

night. Traditional Moroccan pastries, stews, and other foods are offered to the guests. Mint tea is the traditional drink served. Observant Muslims do not drink alcohol.

To prepare a new home for the young couple, guests give household goods such as blankets, bedding, carpets, and even mattresses. These practical gifts are brought to the home as part of a furnishing party several days before the wedding.

Henna

Henna is a reddish-brown dye made from a shrub that grows in North Africa. For more than two thousand years, Moroccan women have been using henna to decorate their bodies. This practice comes from Amazigh culture and is believed to bring God's blessing, or *baraka*. In Morocco, in addition to making women beautiful, some people believe henna symbols protect

Fiancées Fair

As Morocco continues to change and modernize, one aspect of Amazigh daily life remains very much the same. High in the Middle Atlas Mountains men and women live in small, isolated villages. They depend on their livestock and each other for survival. The men and women of these villages need dependable marriage partners who will help them through the long, cold winters when they may be cut off from more populated areas for months at a time. With no place to find spouses near home, each September, when the harvest is over, men and women travel to the village of Imilchil. They arrive by mule, by truck, or on foot. In Imilchil, during a three-day event known as the Fiancées Fair, they seek suitable wives and husbands from among the estimated thirty thousand people who arrive from throughout the mountain region.

This is courtship in a hurry. The women dress in black-and-white striped cloaks, and wear all of their best silver jewelry. Their distinctive headdresses tell an important story. The many women who are divorced or widowed wear a pointed headdress. A woman who has never been married wears a rounded headdress.

As soon as a likely match is made, the couple registers their intentions to their families. The actual marriage ceremony takes place in the home village. If the marriage is not a success, both members of the couple may be back the next year to try again.

against illness and people who might do them harm. The leaves of the henna trees are pounded into a powder that is mixed with water to make a paste. Women use the paste to paint designs on their hands, faces, and feet.

Applying henna patterns is a joyous part of many celebrations and festivals in Morocco. A bride attends a henna party the night before the wedding ceremony. At the ceremony, called Beberiska, the bride is joined by female relatives and friends. During the henna party, the bride's hands and feet are covered with highly detailed patterns. In some parts of Morocco, the soles of the feet are also painted with henna.

Henna is applied as a thick paste. The longer the paste is left on the skin, the longer the design will last.

Henna designs last between ten days and two weeks before they wear off. Female wedding guests are also decorated in henna designs as part of the preparation for the happy event.

A riad provides a peaceful and shady place for people to relax.

Housing

In cities, people tend to live in houses that are right next to one another. Larger, traditional houses, called *riads*, have few windows to the street and instead are built around interior courtyards. Traditionally, these courtyards provided a place for women to relax out of the site of people from outside their families. People from the countryside who have moved to the city tend to end up in *bidonvilles* (French for "tin can cities"), located on the city outskirts. In these areas, people have built shacks out of whatever materials they could find. Many of these homes lack running water.

A Moroccan woman cooks in tagine pots. The shape of the tagine keeps moisture circulating inside the pot, steaming the food.

Outside of the cities, many villages are built on hilltops. As in the cities, the houses tend to be clustered together. Many of the homes are built of stone or adobe (a mixture of clay, sand, and straw). Some of the villages in isolated areas lack electricity.

Food

Moroccan cooks take advantage of the country's best products, especially the country's abundant fresh vegetables, olives, nuts, and spices. These natural flavors add a tantalizing taste to the stew, called a *tagine*, that is at the center of the Moroccan diet. There is no end to the ways these spices, including cinnamon, cardamom, coriander, saffron, and garlic, can be mixed to enhance the flavor of the meats and vegetables that make up a tagine. Carrots and squash are often included in tagines, as are beans. Almonds, dates, prunes, and raisins are typically added, bringing their own sweet flavors. The dish may be made with chicken, lamb, or any meat that is used in slow-cooking recipes.

The tagine is cooked in a special clay pot also called a tagine. It consists of a curved, saucer-shaped bottom with a cone-shaped lid. Tagines are sometimes glazed in colorful patterns. The clay tagine can be used over a charcoal fire, on the stovetop, or in the oven.

A tagine is usually served with couscous, a dish made of a fine type of wheat called semolina. The grain cooks quickly

Celebrating with Food

Dates play such a large a role in the diet of the Moroccan people and in the nation's economy that they have inspired a festival. Every October, after the annual date harvest, villagers from the Draa Valley head to Erfoud, a major date-growing town in the south, to celebrate. Tourists and locals alike enjoy the music and dancing. And everyone eats lots of dates, both dried and as an ingredient in many delicious dishes.

Like dates, almonds are a crucial ingredient in Moroccan cooking, and each year, an almond blossom festival is held in Tafraoute. The town is said to produce more almonds than any other region in Morocco. People from all over come to the red-walled town located in the Anti-Atlas Mountains. The trees, laden with white or pale pink blossoms, form a spectacular backdrop to the events taking place there.

when mixed with boiling water. Couscous is popular throughout North Africa. It is an old Amazigh dish that has been documented as far back as the thirteenth century. Couscous mixes well with the juices and flavors of the tagine.

A Moroccan man pours mint tea. Although women typically do the cooking in Morocco, men prepare and serve the tea.

Another important part of a Moroccan meal is bread, called *khobz* in Moroccan Arabic. The bread is round, crusty, and quite puffy. It is perfect for scooping up the sauce of a tagine.

Breakfast in Morocco typically features pastries. Croissants are common, evidence of the country's long connection with France. Yogurt, dates, olives, cheese, and eggs are also common breakfast foods. For snacks, many Moroccans eat grilled, skewered meats called brochettes. Desserts are usually pastries, often filled with almonds and dripping with honey.

All Moroccan meals are accompanied by sweet mint tea made with fresh mint

National Holidays

New Year's Day	January 1
Independence Manifesto Day	January 11
Labor Day	May 1
Throne Day	July 30
Allegiance Day	August 14
Anniversary of the Revolution of the King and the People	August 20
Youth Day	August 21
Anniversary of the Green March	November 6
Independence Day	November 18

and lots of sugar. The tea is served in glasses. Pouring the tea can be quite dramatic as the server, often a man, holds the teapot high above a tray of glasses and pours from a great height. Guests in a Moroccan home are always offered tea. It is an essential part of the culture.

Today and Tomorrow

Morocco today is a mix of the traditional and the modern. It is not unusual to see a woman in a full body cover riding on the back of a motorcycle. Cell phones are common throughout the country. Only the most remote areas of Morocco remain isolated from modern communications and a steady flow of information. Moroccans are active users of the Internet and social media. Facebook has more than five million users in Morocco. During the Arab Spring, Moroccans used both cell phones and Facebook to communicate information about street protests. Although Morocco is a country with strong cultural traditions, it has fully embraced the tools of twenty-first-century life and is using them to work toward a brighter future.

Fast Facts

Official name: Kingdom of Morocco

Capital: Rabat

Official languages: Arabic, Tamazight

Casablanca

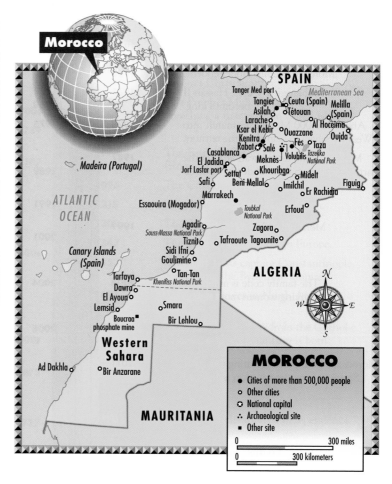

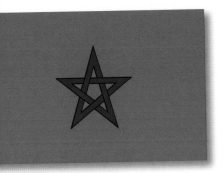

National flag

Rif Mountains

Official religion: Islam

National anthem: Cherifian Anthem

Government: Constitutional monarchy

Head of state: King

Head of government: Prime minister

Area: 170,773 square miles (442,300 sq km)

Area including Western Sahara: 273,773 square miles (709,000 sq km)

Latitude and longitude of geographic center: 32°00' N, 5°00' W

Bordering lands: Algeria to the east and southeast; Western Sahara to the south; the Spanish cities of Ceuta and Melilla to the north

Highest elevation: Mount Toubkal, 13,665 feet (4,165 m)

Lowest elevation: Sebkha Tah, 180 feet (55 m) below sea level

Longest river: Draa, 683 miles (1,100 km)

Average high temperature: In Rabat, 81°F (27°C) in July, 63°F (17°C) in January; in Marrakech, 101°F (38°C) in July, 66°F (19°C) in January

Average low temperature: In Rabat, 64°F (18°C) in July, 45°F (7°C) in January; in Marrakech, 70°F (21°C) in July, 44°F (6°C) in January

Average annual precipitation: In Rabat, 22 inches (56 cm); in Marrakech, 11 inches (28 cm)

Hassan II Mosque

National population (2014 est.): 33,492,909

Population of major cities (2014 est.):

Casablanca	3,145,000
Rabat	1,656,000
Fès	965,000
Salé	903,000
Marrakech	839,000

Landmarks:
- ▶ *Bab Oudaia*, Rabat
- ▶ *Djemma el-Fna*, Marrakech
- ▶ *Hassan II Mosque*, Casablanca
- ▶ *Majorelle Garden*, Marrakech
- ▶ *Tangier American Legation Museum*, Tangier
- ▶ *Volubilis*, near Meknès

Economy: About 40 percent of Moroccans work in agriculture, tending crops such as barley, wheat, dates, olives, oranges, apples, beans, and peas. Phosphate mining is among the nation's most valuable industries. Food processing is the nation's major manufacturing industry. Automobiles, chemicals, iron, and steel are all made in Morocco. In addition, craftspeople make traditional clothing and household items from brass, ceramics, leather, and textiles. Major new port construction near Tangier handles massive containerships. Tourism is a major industry, and the nation attracts about 10 million foreign visitors a year.

Currency

Currency: Moroccan dirham. In 2014, 1 dirham equaled about 11 U.S. cents.

System of weights and measures: Metric system

Schoolchildren

Nawal El Moutawakel

Literacy rate (2011): 67%

Common Arabic words and phrases:

lla	no
iyyeh, n'am	yes
afak	please
shokran	thank you
salam	hello, peace
bslama	good-bye
wakha	okay
daba	now

Prominent Moroccans:

Laila Lalami (1968–)
Novelist

Mawlay Ismail ibn Sharif (1645?–1727)
Leader of the Alawite dynasty

Mohammed V (1909–1961)
(Mohammed Ben Youssef)
First king of Morocco

Mohammed VI (1963–)
King

Nawal El Moutawakel (1962–)
Olympic track-and-field champion

To Find Out More

Books

▶ Hamilton, Richard. *The Last Storytellers: Tales from the Heart of Morocco*. New York: I. B. Tauris, 2013.

▶ Kavanaugh, Dorothy. *Morocco*. Philadelphia: Mason Crest, 2013.

▶ Lappi, Megan. *The Sahara Desert: The Largest Desert in the World*. New York: Weigl, 2006.

▶ Reynolds, Jan. *Sahara*. New York: Lee & Low Books, 2007.

Music

▶ Eddine, Nour. *Morocco Traditional Songs and Music*. West Sussex, UK: ARC Music, 2010.

▶ Master Musicians of Jajouka. *The Master Musicians of Jajouka*. Genes Records, 1995.

▶ Visit this Scholastic Web site for more information on Morocco:
www.factsfornow.scholastic.com
Enter the keyword **Morocco**

Index

Page numbers in *italics*
indicate illustrations.

A

Aben Danan Synagogue, *100*
acacia trees, *32*
Agadir, 25, 103
agriculture
    climate and, 13, 25, 77
    crops, 77, *77*, 81
    dates, 22, 24, *32*, *77*, 78, *78*
    economy and, 77–78, *77*, 81, 125
    employment and, 13, 77
    farmland, 19, *19*, 77
    forests and, 19
    fruit crops, 19, *19*
    government and, 25
    High Atlas Mountains and, 21
    irrigation, 19, 22, 77
    livestock, 78, *104*, 105
    oases, 22, 24, 32
airports, 12, 84
Alawi dynasty, 11, 41–42, 50, 61, 133
Al Hoceima, 25, *75*
Almohad dynasty, 40, *40*, 67
almonds, 125
Almoravid dynasty, 40, *40*
Amazigh people. *See also* people.
    Arab people and, 38, 87–88
    arrival of, 36, 37
    clothing, *116*
    desert regions and, 39, *39*, 52,
        87–88, *116*

    fantasia performances, 119, *119*
    Fiancées Fair, 121, *121*
    French colonization and, 45
    henna and, 120
    independence of, 40
    Islamic religion and, 38, 88
    languages, 90, 91, 92–93, *93*
    Maghreb region and, 87–88
    marriage, 119, 121
    mountain regions and, 40, 87
    music of, 112
    Rif War, 45, *45*
    Spanish colonization and, 52
    tattoos, 89, 120
    women, 89, 121, *121*
Andalusian Gardens, 67
animal life
    Barbary lions, 29, *29*
    Barbary macaques, 28, *29*
    birds, 30–31, *30*, *31*
    camels, 22, 28, *28*, 39, 51, *51*, 78,
        80, 109
    coastline, 30
    deserts, 27, 31, 51
    Egyptian nightjars, 31, *31*
    fennec foxes, 26, 27
    flamingos, *30*
    horses, 78, 109, 119, *119*
    jerboas, 27
    livestock, 78, *104*, 105
    mountains, 28, 29
    national parks, 30, 31
    northern bald ibises, *30*
    zoos, 29
Anti-Atlas Mountains, *20*, 125
Arabic language, 69, 88, 90, *90*, 91,
    92, *92*, 93, 96, 97
Arab people, 38, 87–88, 112
Arab Spring, 12–13, *12*, 55–57, 127
architecture, 10, 23, 75, 76, 92, 97,
    103, *103*, 107

art
    calligraphy, 106
    festivals, 110, *110*
    henna, 73, 120, 122–123, *122*
    Madrassa Ben Youssef, 106
    mosaics, *37*, 38
    murals, 110, *110*
    Museum of Islamic Art, 33, *33*
    Roman Empire and, *37*, 38
    tapestries, *41*, 75
    tilework, 8, 10
Asilah, 110, *110*
Atlantic Ocean, 9, 15, 84
Atlas Mountains, 20–21, *20*, 24, *24*,
    25, 28, 29, 87, 103, 109, 121
Authenticity and Modernity Party, 63
automobile industry, 80, 85

B

Bab Oudaia, 67
banyan trees, 33
Barbary lions, 29, *29*
Barbary macaques, 28, *29*
barite mining, 83
bay'a ceremony, 61–62, *61*
Beberiska ceremony, 122
Ben Arafa, Mohammed, 49
Beni Ourain people, 110
Berbers. *See* Amazigh people.
beverages, 120, 126–127, *126*
bidonvilles ("tin can cities"), 123
birds, 30–31, *30*, *31*
borders, 15, 16
Boucraa, 81
Bou Regreg River, 67
bread, 126
breakfast foods, 126
brochettes (snacks), 126

C

calendar, 101, 102, 104
calligraphy, 106

camels, 22, 28, *28*, 39, 51, *51*, 78, 80, 109
Canary Current, 79
capital city. *See* Rabat.
Casablanca. *See also* cities.
   architecture in, 23, *97*
   automobile industry in, 80
   France and, 23
   Hassan II Mosque, 103, *103*
   manufacturing in, 80
   mosques in, *102*, 103, *103*, 105
   population of, 23, 87
   roadways in, *57*
   sports in, 114
   Tanger Med port, 85, *85*
casbahs (living areas), 42
Ceuta, Spain, 16
chaabi music, 113
Chefchaouen, *76*
chemical industry, 80
Cherifian Anthem, 69
children, 66, 94, *94*, 95–96, 117
Choukri, Mohamed, 110
Chraibi, Driss, 110, *111*
Christianity, 37, 99
Churchill, Winston, 47, *47*
cities. *See also* Casablanca; Fès;
   Marrakech; Rabat; Tangier; towns;
   villages.
   Agadir, 25, 103
   Al Hoceima, 25, *75*
   El Ayoun, 82
   El Jadida, *82*
   Khouribga, 82
   Meknès, 8, 42, *42*
   Salé, 23, 35, 67, 87
   Tan-Tan, 51
   Tarfaya, 20, 50, 53
   Tétouan, *13*
climate, 13, 18, 19, 21, 24–25, 32, 33, 77

clothing, 107, *107*, *116*, 118–119, 121, *121*
coastline, 9, 15, 17, 19, 20, 23, 28, 30, 41, 50, 67, 76, *75*, 89, 103, 110
communications, 61–62, 97, 127
constitution, 13, 57, 59, 61
couscous (food), 125–126
crafts, *74*, *75*, 78, *108*, 109–110
currency (dirham), 80, *80*

D

dance, 119
dates, 22, 24, 32, *77*, 78, *78*, 104, 125, *125*
Deglet Noor dates, 78
dessert foods, 126
dirham (currency), 80, *80*
divorce, 66
djellaba (robe), *116*
Djemma el-Fna, 23, 73, *73*
Draa River, 18

E

earthquakes, 25, *25*, 38
economy
   agriculture, 77–78, 81, 125
   automobile industry, 80, 85
   chemical industry, 80
   currency (dirham), 80, *80*
   employment, 13, *13*, 56, 71, 74–75, *74*, 76, 77, 89, 95, 117
   exports, 71, 78, 81
   fishing industry, 78–79, *79*
   food processing, 80
   government and, 12
   manufacturing, 80, 81, 85
   mining, 54, *54*, 81–83, *82*
   remittances, 71
   textile industry, 44
   tourism, 23, 70, 71, *72*, 73, 74–76, *75*, 85
   trade, 36, 39

transportation and, 84–85, *85*
ecotourism, 76
education, 11–12, 91, *91*, 94–97, *94*, *95*, *96*, *97*, 106–107
Egyptian nightjars, 31, *31*
Eid al-Adha holiday, 104, 105, *105*
Eid al-Fitr holiday, 105
El Ayoun, 82
elections, 54, 57
electricity, 83–84, *84*
El Jadida, 82
El Morabity, Rachid, 115
El Moutawakel, Nawal, 114, *114*
emigration, 99
employment, 13, *13*, 56, 71, 74–75, *74*, 76, 77, 89, 95, 117
Erfoud, 34, 35, 125
European colonization, 43–44, *43*
executive branch of government, 57, 59, 62, 68
exports, 71, 78, 81

F

Facebook, 127
families, 66, *66*, 117
fantasia performances, 119, *119*
fennec foxes, 26, 27
Fès. *See also* cities.
   Aben Danan Synagogue, *100*
   Alawi dynasty and, 42
   families in, 66
   Madrassa Bou Inania, 107, *107*
   murals in, *90*
   population of, 23, 87
   Qarawiyin Mosque, 23
   Qarawiyin University, 94, *94*
   religion in, 23, 98, *100*
   souks in, *72*, *108*
   tourism in, 10–11
Fiancées Fair, 121, *121*
Figuig, 22, *22*, 24
al-Fihri, Fatima, 94

fishing industry, 78–79, *79*
Five Pillars of Islam, 101
flamingos, *30*
food processing, 80
foods, 13, 35, 36–37, 70, 73, 78, 80, *103*, 104–105, *104*, 119–120, 124–127, *124*, *125*
forests, 19, 20–21, 32
fossils, *34*, 35
France
    Amazigh people and, 45, *45*
    Andalusian Gardens and, 67
    architecture and, 23
    Casablanca and, 23
    foods and, 126
    government and, 11, 43–44, 45, 48, 49, 50
    independence and, 48–49, 50
    language and, 89, 91, *91*
    Mohammed V and, 49, 50
    Rabat and, 67
    Rif War and, 45, *45*
    tourism and, 75
    World War II and, 46

G

gardens, 33, *33*
geography
    borders, 15, 16
    coastline, 9, 15, 17, 19, 20
    desert, 9, *14*, 15, 17, 19, 21, *21*
    elevation, 17, 18, 19–20
    land area, 15, 18
    mountains, 15, 17, *17*, 18, *18*, 19, 20–21, *20*, 24, *24*, 25
    oases, 22, *22*, 24
    plains, 19
    rivers, *17*, 18, 19
    sand dunes, 21, *21*
Germany, 43, 46, 50
ginbri (musical instrument), *112*
government
    agriculture and, 25
    Alawi dynasty, 11, 41–42, 50, 61
    Almohad dynasty, 40, *40*
    Almoravid dynasty, 40, *40*
    Arab Spring and, 57
    Authenticity and Modernity Party, 63
    bay'a ceremony, 61–62, *61*
    constitution, 13, 57, 59, 61
    economy and, 12
    education and, 11–12
    elections, 54, 57
    executive branch, 57, 59, 62, 68
    French colonization, 11, 43–44, 45, 48, 49, 50
    Hassan II, 11, 49, 52, *53*, 54, 60, 64, 67
    House of Councillors, 63
    House of Representatives, 63
    Idrisid dynasty, 39, *40*
    independence, 11, 48–49, *48*, *49*, 50
    Istiqlal Party, 48, *48*, 63
    judicial branch, 62, 64, *64*
    Justice and Development Party, 63
    language and, 89, 91
    legislative branch, 54, 59, 62, 63, *63*, 65
    Marinid dynasty, 40, *40*
    military, 46, 53, *55*, 62
    mining and, 82–83
    Mohammed Ben Arafa, 49
    Mohammed Laghdaf, 51
    Mohammed V, 45, 47, *47*, 49, 50, *50*, 60, 67, 133
    Mohammed VI, 11–12, 13, 54, *55*, 57, *58*, 60–61, *60*, 65, *65*, 80, *80*, 84, 133
    Mudawana (family code), 64–66, 68
    National Rally of Independents, 63
    Parliament, 54, 59, 65
    political parties, 48, *48*, 59, 63
    Portuguese and, 40–41
    prime ministers, 57, 59, 62
    religion and, 99
    Spain and, 11, 48, 50, 53
    transportation and, 12
    tribal chiefs, 51
    United States and, 43
    women and, 63, 68
Great Britain, 47, *47*
Green March, 52–53, *52*

H

Hakkaoui, Bassima, 68
Halawi dates, 78
Hassan II, 11, 49, 52–53, *53*, 54, 60, 64, 67
Hassan II Bridge, 67
Hassan II Mosque, 103, *103*
Hassan III, 65
henna, 73, 120, 122–123, *122*
High Atlas Mountains, 20–21
Hijrah (migration), 101
hip-hop music, 113
historical maps. *See also* maps.
    Colonial Morocco (1923), 43
    Dynasties, *40*
    Western Sahara, 53
holidays
    national, 60, 127
    religious, 104–105
horses, 78, 109, 119, *119*
House of Councillors, 63
House of Representatives, 63
housing, 38, 120, 123–124, *123*
Houssaini, Ali Sqalli, 69
hurricanes, 42

I

Idris I, 38–39
Idris II, 39
Idrisid dynasty, 39, *40*
Ifni province, 50

Iguider, Abdalaati, 114
Imilchil, 121
independence, 11, 48–49, *48*, *49*, 50
inheritance, 68
International Court of Justice, 52
International Zone, 44
Internet, 97, 127
irrigation, 19, 22, 77
Islamic religion. *See also* religion.
　Alawi family and, 61
　alcohol and, 120
　Almoravid dynasty, 40
　Amazigh people and, 38, 88
　architecture and, 10
　calendar, 101, 102, 104
　Eid al-Adha holiday, *104*, 105, *105*
　Eid al-Fitr holiday, 105
　fasting, 103–104
　Five Pillars of Islam, 101
　Green March and, 53
　Hassan II Mosque, 103, *103*
　Hijrah (migration), 101
　holidays, 104–105
　kings and, 61, 62
　Koutoubia Mosque, 23
　madrassas (religious schools),
　　106–107, *107*
　Mecca, Saudi Arabia, 99, 101, 102,
　　104
　Medina, Saudi Arabia, 101, 104
　minaret (mosque tower), 102, *102*,
　　103, *103*
　Mosque el-Atiqa, 67
　mosques, 62, 67, 98, 102, *102*, 103,
　　103, 105, *105*
　moussem festivals, 119
　muezzin (prayer caller), 102, *102*
　Muhammad (prophet), 50, 61,
　　99–100, 101, 102, 104
　Museum of Islamic Art, 33, *33*
　national flag and, 60, *60*
　origins of, 37, 99–101

prayer, 62, 101, *101*, 102, *102*, 105,
　105, 107
　Qarawiyin Mosque, 23
　Qur'an (holy book), 53, 100, 106,
　　106, 107
　Ramadan (holy month), 102–105
　Shia Muslims, 101
　Sunni Muslims, 101
　women and, 102, *103*, 107, *107*
　wudu ritual, 98
Ismail ibn Sharif, Mawlay, 42, *42*, 133
Istiqlal Party, 48, *48*, 63

J
jerboas, 27
Jorf Lasfar port, 82
Judaism, 37, 44, *76*, 99, *100*
judicial branch of government, 62,
　64, *64*
Justice and Development Party, 63

K
khobz (bread), 126
Khouribga, 82
Kimball, Nikki, 115
Koutoubia Mosque, 23

L
Laghdaf, Mohammed, 51
Lalami, Laila, 111, 133
Lalla Salma (princess), 65
languages, 69, 88, 89, 90–93, *90*, *91*,
　92, *93*, 96
Laou River, *17*
leather, 73, *73*, 78
legation building, 43, *43*
legislative branch of government, 54,
　59, 62, 63, *63*, 65
literacy rate, 96
literature, 110–111, *111*, 133
livestock, 78, *104*, 105

M
madrassas (religious schools), 106–
　107, *107*
Maghreb region, 87–88
Majorelle Garden, 33, *33*
Majorelle, Jacques, 33
manufacturing, 80, 81, 85
maps. *See also* historical maps.
　geopolitical, *10*
　population density, 88
　Rabat, 67
　resources, 83
　topographical, *18*
Marathon des Sables (Marathon of
　the Sands), 115, *115*
marine life, 28–29, *34*, 35, 78–79, *79*
Marinid dynasty, 40, *40*
marketplaces. *See* souks.
Marrakech. *See also* cities.
　Alawi dynasty and, 42
　climate in, 18
　Djemma el-Fna, 23, 73, *73*
　Koutoubia Mosque, 23
　Madrassa Ben Youssef, 106
　Majorelle Garden, 33, *33*
　Mellah (Jewish quarter), 23
　population of, 23, 86, 87
　souks, *11*, *70*
　street musicians, *112*
　tanneries, 73, *73*
　tourism in, 10–11
marriage, 66, 68, 118–120, *118*, 121,
　122
Master Musicians of Jajouka, 112–113
Mausoleum of Mohammed V, 67
Mecca, Saudi Arabia, 99, 101, 102,
　104
medinas, 72
Medina, Saudi Arabia, 101, 104
Mediterranean Sea, 9, 15, 16, 17
Medjool dates, 78
Meknès, 8, 42, *42*

Melilla, Spain, 16

Mellah (Jewish quarter), 23

Mendoubia Gardens, 33, *33*

migrant workers, 16, *16*

military, *46*, 53, *55*, 62

minarets (mosque towers), 102, *102*, 103, *103*

mining, 54, *54*, 81–83, *82*

mint tea, 120, 126–127, *126*

Mogador settlement, 37

Mohammed III, 43

Mohammed V, 45, 47, *47*, 49, 50, *50*, 60, 67, 133

Mohammed V International Airport, 84

Mohammed V University, 95, *95*

Mohammed VI, 11–12, *13*, 54, *55*, 57, *58*, 60–61, *60*, 65, *65*, 80, *80*, 84, 133

monk seals, 29

Morgan, Léo, 69

mosaics, *37*, 38

Mosque el-Atiqa, 67

mosques, 62, 67, 98, 102, *102*, 103, *103*, 105, *105*

Mount Bou Nasser, 20

Mount Tidirhine, 17

Mount Toubkal, 18, 20

moussem festivals, 119

El Moutawakel, Nawal, 133, *133*

Mudawana (family code), 64–66, 68

muezzin (prayer caller), 102, *102*

Muhammad (Islamic prophet), 50, 61, 99–100, 101, 102, 104

murals, *90*, 110, *110*

Museum of Islamic Art, 33

museums, 33, 43

music, 69, 112–113, *112*, 119, 120

Muslim (hip-hop musician), 113

N

national anthem, 69

national flag, 60, *60*, 69

national holidays, 60, 127

national parks, 30, 31

National Rally of Independents, 63

national symbol, 29, *29*

Neo-Tifinagh language, 93

nomads, 51, 52

northern bald ibises, *30*

O

oases, 22, *22*, 24, 32, 35, 39, 87

Olympic Games, 114, *114*, 133, *133*

overfishing, 79

P

Parliament, 54, 59, 65

Patton, George, 46

people. *See also* Amazigh people; women.

    Alawis, 11, 41–42, 50, 61, 133

    Almohads, 40, *40*, 67

    Almoravids, 40, *40*

    ancestors, 36

    Arabs, 38, 87–88, 112

    Beni Ourain, 110

    children, 66, 94, *94*, 95–96, 117

    clothing, 107, *116*, 118–119, 121, *121*

    divorce, 66

    education, 11–12, 91, *91*, 94–97, *94*, *96*, *97*, 106–107

    emigration, *13*, 95, 99

    employment, 13, *13*, 56, 71, 74–75, *74*, 76, 89, 95, 117

    families, 66, *66*, 117

    foods, 13, 35, 36–37, 70, 73, 78, 80, *103*, 104–105, *104*, 119–120, 124–127, *124*, *125*

    hospitality of, 127

    housing, 38, 120, 123–124, *123*

    Idrisids, 39, *40*

    inheritance, 68

    languages, 69, 88, 89, 90–93, *90*, *91*, *92*, 93, 96

    literacy rate, 96

    Marinids, 40, *40*

    marriage, 66, 68, 118–120, *118*, 121, 122

    migrant workers, 16, *16*

    Mudawana (family code), 64–66, 68

    nomads, 51, 52

    Phoenicians, 36–37, *36*, 44

    population, 16, 23, 44, 86, 87, 88, 110

    Portuguese, 40–41, *41*

    prehistoric people, 35

    Romans, 37, *37*, 38, *38*, 67

    Sahrawis, 51

    tattoos, 73, 89, 120, 122–123, *122*

Phoenician people, 36–37, *36*, 44, 67

phosphate mining, 54, *54*, 81–83, *82*

pirates, 23

plant life

    acacia trees, *32*

    agriculture and, 19

    banyan trees, 33

    climate and, 32, 33

    dates, 22, 24, 32, 77, 78, *78*, 104, 125, *125*

    deserts, 32

    forests, 19, 20–21, 32

    gardens, 33, *33*

    scrublands, 32

political parties, 48, *48*, 59, 63

pollution, 83

population, 16, 23, 44, 67, 86, 87, 88, 110

ports, 17, 23, 25, 42, 44, 67, 80, 81, 82, 84–85, *85*

Portuguese people, 40–41, *41*

pottery, 23, *74*

prehistoric people, 35

prime ministers, 57, 59, 62

Q

Qarawiyin Mosque, 23
Qarawiyin University, 94, *94*
Qur'an (Islamic holy book), 53, 100, 106, *106*, 107

R

Rabat. *See also* cities.
Almohad dynasty, 67
Andalusian Gardens, 67
Bab Oudaia, 67
climate of, 18, 24
France and, 67
Hassan II Bridge, 67
judicial branch in, *64*
Laila Lalami and, 111
legislative branch in, *63*
location of, 67
map of, 67
Mausoleum of Mohammed V, 67
Mohammed V University, 95, *95*
name origin, 67
Phoenicians in, 67
population of, 23, 67, 87
Roman Empire in, 67
souks in, *103*
railways, 84
rai music, 113
Ramadan (Islamic holy month), 102–105
al-Rashid, Mawlay, 41–42
religion. *See also* Islamic religion.
Christianity, 37, 99
government and, 99
Judaism, 37, 44, 76, 99, *100*
remittances, 71
Renault cars, 80
riads (housing), 123, *123*
Rif Mountains, 15, 17, *17*, 18, 19, 76, 87, 113
Rif War, 45, *45*
roadways, 12, *57*, 84

Roman Empire, 37, *37*, 38, *38*, 67
Roosevelt, Franklin D., 46–47, *47*
rugs, *108*, 109–110

S

Sahara Desert
Almoravid dynasty in, 40
Amazigh people in, 39, *39*, 52, 87–88, *116*
animal life in, 27, 31, 51
climate of, 17, 18, 19
dunes, 21, *21*
Green March and, 52–53, *52*
Hassan II and, 52–53
High Atlas Mountains and, 21
Marathon des Sables (Marathon of the Sands), 115, *115*
Mohammed Laghdaf and, 51
oases in, 22, *22*, 24, 32, 35, 39, 87
phosphate mining in, 54, *54*, 81, 82, 83
plant life in, 32
Rif Mountains and, 17, 19
size of, 9, *14*, 15
solar energy and, 83
Spain and, 44, 50, 52, *52*
trade routes, 39, *39*
wall in, 53–54, *54*
Sahrawi people, 51
Salé, 23, 35, 67, 87
salt, 36–37
Scramble for Africa, 43
scrublands, 32
Sebkha Tah, 18, 19–20
Sebou River, 19, *19*
Shia Muslims, 101
snack foods, 126
soccer, 113, *113*
solar energy, 83–84
Souissi, 95
souks (marketplaces), *11*, 70, 72, *72*, 74, *103*, 108

Souss-Massa National Park, 30, 31
Spain, 11, 16, 43, *43*, 44, 45, 48, 50, 52, 53, 75, 79, 89
Spanish language, 89, 91
Spanish Sahara, 44, 50, 52, *52*
spices, *11*, 124–125
sports, 113–114, *113*, *114*, *115*, 133, *133*
Strait of Gibraltar, 9, 85
Sunni Muslims, 101

T

Tafilalt (oasis), 24
Tafraoute, 103, 125
tagine (pots), *124*, 125
tagine (stew), 124–125, *124*, 126
Tamazight language, 90, 97
Tanger Med port, 85, *85*
Tangier. *See also* cities.
automobile manufacturing in, 80
France and, 44
International Zone and, 44
legation building, 43, *43*
manufacturing in, 80
Melloussa suburb, 80
Mendoubia Gardens, 33, *33*
Mohamed Choukri and, 110
museums in, 43
Phoenicians in, 44
population of, 44
Rif Mountains and, 17
tourism in, 10–11
tanneries, 73, *73*
Tan-Tan, 51
Tan Tan Moussem, 51, *51*
tapestries, *41*, 75
Tarfaya, 20, 50, 53
tattoos, 73, 89, 120, 122–123, *122*
television, 61–62
Tétouan, *13*
textile industry, 44
tile work, 8, 10

tourism, 10–11, 23, 70, 71, *72*, 73, 74–76, *75*, 85
towns. *See also* cities; villages.
   Boucraa, 81
   Chefchaouen, 76
   Erfoud, *34*, 35, 125
   Figuig, 22, *22*, 24
   Tafraoute, 103, 125
trade, 36, 39, *39*
transportation, 12, 84–85, *85*
tribal chiefs, 51
trilobites, *34*, 35

U
ultramarathons, 115, *115*
unemployment, 13
United States, 43, 46–47, 76, 81, 104, 115

V
villages. *See also* cities; towns.
   Asilah, 110, *110*
   Imilchil, 121
Volubilis (ruins), *37*, 38, *38*

W
water, 19, 22, 33, 35, 77
weaving, 75, 110
Western Sahara Desert, 15, 44, 50, 52, *52*, 53–54, *53*, *54*, *82*
wildlife. *See* animal life; marine life; plant life.
wind energy, 84, *84*
women. *See also* people.
   Amazighs, 89, 121, *121*
   clothing and, 107, *107*
   education and, 95, *95*, 96, *96*
   executive branch and, 68
   Fiancées Fair, 121, *121*
   Islamic religion and, 102, *105*, 107, *107*
   legislative branch and, 63
   marriage, 68, 121

   Mohammed VI and, 54
   rights of, *56*, 68
   sports and, 114, *114*
World Cup soccer tournament, 113
World War II, 46–47, *46*
wudu ritual, 98

Z
zoos, 29

Meet the Authors

ETTAGALE BLAUER HAS BEEN TRAVELING TO Morocco since 1969, when she began a journey across Africa in Asilah, Morocco. She warded off the chilly nights in the Sahara wearing a warm hooded robe called a *djellaba* that she bought in Rabat. Through many trips to Morocco and the Sahara, she experienced the cultures of Morocco, enjoyed the delicious foods, explored the mazelike medinas, and tried out her college French. The Moroccans she met were always delighted to try out their English and explain their ceremonies, their history, and their cultures. In the years since, she has returned to Morocco many times. Blauer has traveled all around Africa and has lived in Kenya and South Africa.

Jason Lauré made his first trip across the Sahara in 1970. He made his way into the Moroccan Sahara on roads that were little more than rock-strewn paths, but experienced the beautiful and varied landscapes of Morocco. He has returned to Morocco time after time, venturing into the most desolate parts of the Sahara as well as the teeming medinas. Lauré lives in Cape Town, South Africa.

Photo Credits